Martyn Whittock \
Head of Humaniti
has written, or co-written, eignt history textbooks and three medieval historical novels. He has acted as a historical consultant to the BBC and National Trust and is a Methodist Lay Preacher and Anglican Lay Reader. He lives on the Wiltshire-Somerset border with his wife and two daughters, within the 10 mile radius in which his family have lived for 500 years.

Following page
A reconstruction by Alan Sorrell of King Alfred's palace at Cheddar, and where he probably entertained the Viking king, Guthrum, after his baptism at Aller.
[see Walk 7]

Walking
SOMERSET
History

MARTYN WHITTOCK

Photographs by Julian Comrie
Maps by Angela Ewing

THE DOVECOTE PRESS

To Esther Grace Whittock, with love.

First published in 1995 by the Dovecote Press Ltd
Stanbridge, Wimborne, Dorset BH21 4JD

ISBN 1 874336 31 8

© Martyn Whittock

Phototypeset by the Typesetting Bureau
Wimborne, Dorset
Printed and bound by Biddles Ltd,
Guildford and Kings Lynn

Contents

Introduction

Somerset is a wonderful county to walk in. From the bleak uplands of Exmoor, to the Mendip and Quantock Hills, or the flat low-lying Levels that fill the heart of the county, Somerset offers a range of landscapes that each bears the imprint of its history and has been shaped by mans' efforts to settle and cultivate it. For this is more than a book of walks; it also takes you backwards through time.

Each of the fifteen walks focuses on a particular period in Somerset's past, with a theme that connects and guides the whole of the walk. The difference, of course, between this and a purely written history is that in a book of walks it is possible to actually visit the places where that history was made. How much easier to understand the Battle of Sedgemoor by walking the battlefield, or Somerset's lead, cloth and coal trades by visiting the areas where they flourished.

The walks are arranged in chronological order. The first takes us to some of the intriguing prehistoric sites that survive on the Mendips and Exmoor, the last includes nineteenth century industrial remains on the estuary of the River Parrett and a view of Hinkley Point nuclear power station. I have tried to explain the reasons for the appearance of the countryside through which the walks pass, linking it wherever possible to their historical themes.

The walks have been chosen so as to provide as broad a selection as possible of the different landscapes that give Somerset its character. They are scattered right across the county: perhaps more so than usual, for I have chosen to stay loyal to Somerset's pre-1974 boundaries.

Each walk is accompanied by a map and detailed instructions. A useful companion, though, is an Ordnance Survey 1:25,000 map. These are excellent maps for any walker and are well worth the price. The 1:50,000 Ordnance Survey maps are adequate, but lack the detail and depth of information.

All of the walks are circular and, where possible, start and end in a village or town. In the introduction to each there is outline information on the starting point, facilities, and any problems that might be encountered. Mileages are given, as is a rough indication of the time each walk will take if enjoyed at a modest pace with occasional halts to look at the places visited. Every effort has been made to make them as accessible as possible to people of varying fitness and levels of experience: they are not arduous hikes, nor were they intended to be.

The walks have been 'tested in the field' and public rights of way were correct at the time of publication. I wish you happy and stimulating walking, and hope that you find these journeys into Somerset's past as fascinating and enjoyable as I have.

I would like to thank Dr Robert Dunning (Editor, Victoria County History, Somerset), Chris Webster (Somerset County Council Sites and Monuments Record Officer) and Veryan Heal (Exmoor National Park Archaeologist) for help and advice while planning these walks; Robin Bush for reading part of the text; and my father, Jeff Whittock, and my wife, Chris, for walking them with me – come rain or shine!

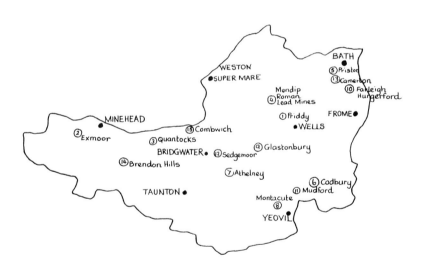

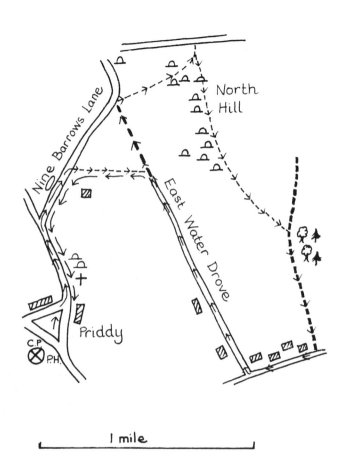

North
Hill

Nine Barrows Lane

East Water Drove

Priddy

C.P.
⊗ P.H.

|—————— 1 mile ——————|

→ →   Route Directions

....   Footpath

-----   Track / Bridleway

⌓ ⌓   Burial mounds / cairns

═══   Roads and Lanes

C.P.   Car Park

P.H.   Public House

⊐⊏⊏⊏   Railway

⊗   Parking Place at start of walk

Stone Age Circles and Bronze Age Burials

Priddy – East Water drove – Priddy Circles
Priddy Nine Barrows – St Catherine's mine
East Water drove – Priddy.

A walk of just under five miles crossing the high country on the top of the Mendip hills. It starts and ends in the village of Priddy and explores some of the prehistoric remains in the area.

Time: Two and a half hours.

Starting Point: The village green at Priddy. (Grid ref: 527 509)

Facilities: Priddy has two excellent pubs, the New Inn on the green itself and the Queen Victoria on the Wookey Hole road out of the village

Problems: The walk is a straightforward one over open countryside. However, some sections can be fairly wet after rain.

Background: The walk starts in Priddy, an important medieval settlement on the Mendips, where a sheep fair has been held since the 14th century. The village was also a centre for lead mining, which continued until 1908. Most significantly for this walk, it was once settled and farmed during the Neolithic period and Bronze Age (from about 4000 to 700 BC).

The size and number of the prehistoric remains around Priddy show that a fairly large population must have been responsible for building and using them. We do not know what these people believed, but the sites must have been important because their contruction would have required a huge amount of time, labour and skill.

The walk offers a contrast between shady lanes and green droves and open hillsides on Mendip top. It also has excellent views, not only of the Mendips around Priddy but, on its higher sections, over the Somerset moors and beyond.

Directions
Start near the Green. There is parking space near the New Inn and across the Green, where cavers park for Swildon's Hole pothole.

Facing the Green from the New Inn, follow the road towards the church on the ridge.

The Green is the site of the sheep fair, which is held here on the nearest Wednesday to August 21st. According to local tradition it was moved here from Wells in 1348, during the Black Death. The pile of hurdles are a symbolic reminder of the fair and are thatched with wheat-straw, which is held in place by hazel spars. Note how they are pushed upwards into the rick to avoid rain running into the thatch. Legend says that should the hurdles ever vanish from the Green then so will Priddy itself.

As you leave the Green, a plaque on the right records how a pipe first brought pure water to Priddy in October 1865. It was paid for by the lord of the manor, James Green.

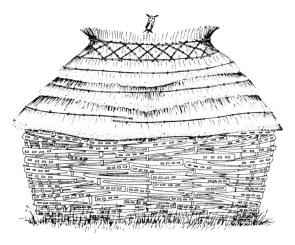

Priddy, hurdle stack.

Walk up the hill to the sign pointing right to the 'Church, School, Village Hall'. Follow it to the church. This can be reached either across a field, via two stone stiles, or via a lane beside the school.

Priddy church has a large churchyard and the fields beside it contain two prehistoric burial mounds. Like the ones we visit later on this walk they date from the earlier Bronze Age (about 2000 – 1000 BC). The one to the west is in a field called Gill's Croft; the one to the north was excavated by the vicar of Priddy in 1895. The church of St Laurence dates from at least the 13th century. Inside, on the north wall, is a 15th century pall, or cloth used to cover the altar. It was lost and then rediscovered in a local farmhouse earlier this century.

Return to the road. Turn right and follow it to the sign 'Nine Bar-rows Lane'. Turn right into the lane. Follow it down hill, past a pond on the left. At the next metal gate on the right after the pond, turn onto a track and follow it to the Bristol Waterworks pumping station. Cross the stone stile to the left of the small brick building. Walk ahead and to the left across the field, using the causeway to cross a small stream, to the next stile, in a hedge. Go diagonally left across this field, to a gateway and keeping a dead tree on your left. At the gateway cross to the wooden stile immediately ahead of you. You are now on East Water drove. Turn left and follow it until it meets the metalled road of Nine Barrow Lane again.

As with many of the droves, or green ways on Mendip, East Water Drove is an ancient track used for the movement of livestock across the open top of the hills. At the metalled road there is a stile on the right. Cross it into the field. Walk to the telegraph pole ahead and to the left, on the ridge.

At the pole, which is beside a quarried area, look left down onto the remains of two round barrows. There are better examples yet to come. There are also magnificent views.

Keep the line of telegraph poles to your right and make for the metal gate, diagonally left across the field. Watch the wet ground! Go through the gate and to the road. Cross the road and look into the opposite field.

The banks and ditches, marked by horse jumps, are called Priddy Circles and they run away from you to the north-north-east. In all there are three circular banks of earth and a fourth, incomplete one, beyond the B3134 road. These kinds of circles are called henges. These were probably centres for religious celebrations and tribal meetings. They probably date from about 2000 BC. Excavations in the 1960s show that the banks are made of earth and turf, faced with stones. Post holes show there was some kind of gate, or wooden monument at each entrance.

Recross the road, back to the gate and into the field again. There is a row of eight burial mounds ahead on the skyline. Walk to the tele-graph pole ahead and left and onto the barrows.

These are burial mounds, like the two by the churchyard and are called Ashen Hill Barrows. Excavations in the early 19th century, by Rev. Skinner of Camerton (see Walk 13) showed that the mounds covered cremations. There are a large number of these barrows around Priddy. The name 'barrow' is from the Old English word 'beorg', meaning both burial mound and hill. These barrows show

Ashen Hill Barrows, with two of the Priddy Nine Barrows in the top left hand corner.

that the area here continued to be an important religious centre well into the Bronze Age. The people buried in the barrows around Priddy were probably the wealthy leaders of their communities, and one of the barrows contained a rare grooved bronze dagger and a decorated pin that had been buried with the body.

Pass through the line of barrows. Aim for the barrow in the corner of the field, where the fence and wall meet.

There are two more burial mounds here. These are part of the barrow cemetery called Priddy Nine Barrows and were first recorded with this name ('Nigheberwes') in 1296. The dip in the top of the second barrow shows it has been robbed of its contents. The rest of the Nine Barrows group is ahead of you and to the left.

Cross the stile ahead of you and follow the wall, keeping it on your right. At the top of the ridge the line of barrows on the right almost meets the line of the wall. The ground on your side of the wall is pitted from old quarrying.

Look back down this line of barrows. The third barrow back has been very badly damaged. Many barrows were ruthlessly dug into in the 19th century, but as far back as the Anglo-Saxon times there were legends of treasure buried in barrows and so they have always attracted robbers. The dry stone wall is the parish boundary between Priddy and Chewton Mendip parishes. The Nine Barrows are often mentioned on medieval and later surveys because they mark this boundary

Far ahead is the TV transmitter above Wells. To the right are superb views to Glastonbury Tor and beyond. Follow the wall downhill. Cross the stile in the right corner of the field. Keep following the wall on your right. There is rough ground, with gorse and bracken, on your left. Cross the stream in the gully and walk onto the track. Turn right and follow the track over a causeway between the lake and disturbed ground on the left and marshy land on the right.

This track is crossing the remains of the St Catherine's lead mine, the last one to work on Mendip and whose closure in 1908 ended an industry dating from pre-Roman times. Around the edge of the lake and ahead of you is a 'gruffy ground', an area where old lead mining pits have collapsed and where slag heaps are now covered with grass. The Stockhill plantation, across the road, covers more of the 'gruffy ground'. Note the shiny lead slag in the track and the spoil heaps to the right. As the path bends to the right, look left and down. There is a quarry face and three parallel mine shafts, with dry-stone-walls, sloping into the bank. These are very dangerous and should NOT be entered. Away to the left the roof has been dug out and the three shafts can be seen, about 6m below. Again, this is a dangerous area and should NOT be entered!

Follow the track to the metalled road and turn right. Pass four houses on the right and 150 metres after the last (called Fairladywell Cottage) turn off the road onto a lane marked 'No Through Road' and 'East Water Lane'. Walk up the lane past farms and the Wessex Caving Club on the left. After the last building, on the right, the metalled road gives way to a track.

It is marked 'Byway RUPP'. Proceed along this track – which is East Water Drove – passing an abandoned lime kiln on the right. Some 50 metres beyond the kiln there is a wooden stile in the wall on the left. You have now come full circle. Retrace your steps across the fields to the pumping station and Nine Barrows Lane. Turn left at the metalled road of the lane and follow the road back to Priddy.

Another place of interest:

Ebbor Gorge, owned by the National Trust, is a beautifully secret place and easily reached from Priddy. Drive out of the village on the Wookey Hole road. After one and a half miles the road bears left and soon you come to a view-point and a car park on the left. From here, well marked footpaths take you down into the gorge itself. It is well worth the visit after the Priddy walk.

Stone Age Hunters sheltered in the gorge as long ago as 12,000 BC. Their stone tools have been found here. At this time scattered hunting bands followed reindeer, red deer and horses across the cold tundra on the top of Mendip and through the willow and birch scrub, lower down the slopes. After about 8000 BC the climate grew warmer and the gorge would then have been covered with thick deciduous woodland.

Looking towards Dunkery Beacon, Exmoor.

Exmoor Barrows and Cairns

Rowbarrows – Dunkery Beacon – Kit Barrows – Joaney How cairns
Cloutsham – Dunkery Beacon – Rowbarrows

A walk of 9 miles, including the highest point on Exmooor (and in Somerset), superb views of Exmoor and the Brendon Hills, and some of Exmoor's intriguing prehistoric barrow cemeteries.

Time: four and a half hours.

Starting point: Wilmersham Common, on the road from Exford to Luccombe, via Exford Common and Stoke Pero Common. (Grid ref: 861 411).

Facilities: None at the starting point, but within 2 miles at Exford there are facilities including pubs and a Youth Hostel.

Problems: None. Although the way includes open moorland it is accessible and makes for good walking. There is a stretch of road walking but the roads in question are not busy.

Background: Exmoor is formed from sandstone rocks and has fairly poor soil. This lack of fertility has been made worse by the high level of rainfall. However, the sites visited on the walk remind us that in prehistoric times the moor had a higher population than today – even if many of those who used it were animal-herding nomads with only temporary shelters on, or near, the moor. The earth-covered burial mounds, stone cairns, and standing stones on the moor are evidence of their presence. They settled on the moor either because an increase in population in the Bronze Age made it necessary to farm more marginal areas, or because the climate was more favourable then.

Directions
Park where the road crossing Exford Common divides (to the left to West Luccombe, to the right to Luccombe). At the divide a track leaves the road on the right. Follow this track, which is a bridleway. Walking westward away from the road the track slowly climbs towards Dunkery Beacon. On the right the moor has been enclosed in fields. Watch out for wet patches further away from the path. The vegetation here is bracken, forest grass and ling but there are patches of spotted orchids, sundew, campunala and bog pimpernel.

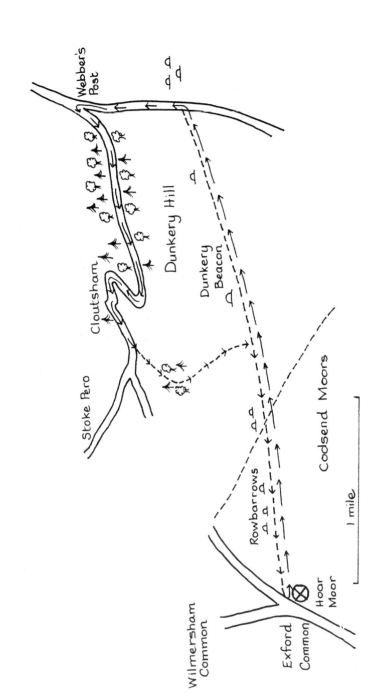

Webber's Post

Dunkery Hill

Cloutsham

Stoke Pero

Dunkery Beacon

Codsend Moors

Rowbarrows

Wilmersham Common

Exford Common

Hoar Moor

1 mile

After about half a mile a series of five round barrows follow the ridge, which is on the left. The first is the great stony mound of Great Rowbarrow. There are then two smaller barrows, one of which is also a cairn of stones. This cairn is called White Barrow. The other is a low mound, covered by heather, and the bank around it suggests that it may have been a type of round barrow called a saucer barrow. The surroundings here are now beautiful but bleak and it is hard to imagine once thriving communities living near here and building these monuments.

Beyond this, to the east lies Little Rowbarrow. It is a heather and grass covered mound, with a small heap of stones on top and, like Great Rowbarrow, was originally a stone cairn. When the mounds were first built they would have looked more impressive, as they would then have been larger and not covered with vegetation.

Sheep still graze the rough pasture, allowing us an idea of how Bronze Age farmers used the moor. They were probably livestock herders who visited the moor in the summer months. The barrows and cairns probably mark the graves of the chieftains of these tribes-people, and may even indicate the edges of grazing territories. Deeper on the moor are the remains of some of the settlements of these early farmers.

As the track passes Little Rowbarrow on the left, the line of enclosed fields on the right falls away to the right but you go straight on, walking towards the beacon. In May and June, look out for the pale pink flowers of crowberry beside the path. Stop when you reach Dunkery Beacon; the view is superb in all directions.

Dunkery Beacon.

Dunkery Beacon is Exmoor's highest point, rising to 1,705 feet. A map of 1687 shows a tower here, but there is no evidence that one actually existed. The name probably means 'rocky hill' (from the Old English 'dun', hill, and Welsh 'creic', rocks. It may contain the Welsh word 'din', hillfort.) Scattered around the summit are the remains of cairns and barrows, now wrecked. Beacon fires have been lit on the summit since the Middle Ages. It is likely that the barrows and cairns were placed high up here as a mark of ownership, since they could be seen from a great distance. It is also possible that they were placed here so that the ancestors could watch over the maximum amount of territory used by the local tribes: a further reminder of how important the moor was in the Bronze Age.

Dunkery is now part of the 12,500 acres of the Holnicote Estate of the National Trust and is a Scheduled Ancient Monument. The current stone cairn here was built in 1935 to commemorate the gift of Dunkery Hill to the Trust. It is built on top of a Bronze Age burial mound, which has been eroded by 30 inches between 1935 and 1993, when 160 tonnes of local stone and 140 tonnes of river gravel were needed to get it back to its original height. This erosion was caused by visitors and a rainfall of over 70 inches per year.

The high rainfall has helped reduce the fertility of the soil on the moor. It may have been the start of this wetter, colder climate which drove the Bronze Age farmers off the moor, leaving their settlements to decay but whose burial barrows remain a memorial to their presence.

Walk on from the beacon, following the track forward and left, towards the road just under 1 mile ahead. As you cross the moor more round barrows, called the Kit Barrows, are on the left. On reaching the road, turn left and follow it.

To the right of the road the mounds of Joaney How Cairns are visible on the summit and north side of the hill. The largest cairn, on top of the hill, is called the Beacon. To its north-west is the cairn known as Robin How and to the north-east is Joaney How cairn, which is surrounded by a ditch. Down the hill there are other cairns, more difficult to make out in the grass and heather. The names of Robin and Joaney cairns are first mentioned in 1889 and might preserve a local legend of the popular medieval outlaws, Robin Hood and Little John. Local legend says the names were made up in the 19th century to fox the surveyor from the Ordnance Survey!

Walk down the metalled road, for just over 1 mile, to the junction at Webber's Post.

Circular enclosure at Cloutsham, below Dunkery Beacon.

At Webber's Post the tree lined hills to the north and west are a contrast to the moorland you have left behind. Horner Wood, to the west, is a rare ancient oak woodland of 900 acres, rich in rare lichens. At least 165 species have been found here, compared to 100 in what is usually regarded as a good example of ancient woodland. It is also home to fritillary butterflies, pied flycatchers, dippers and red deer. In 1994 remains of settlements dating from the Iron Age to the Middle Ages were discovered in the wood, a further reminder that the edges of the moor have supported higher populations in the past than now. The settlement in Horner Wood remained long after those on the open moor had been abandoned, and it is likely that what is now regarded as ancient oak woodland was once largely cleared of trees. The present woodland probably regrew after the settlements declined.

Turn left at Webber's Post, taking the road that soon runs through woodland towards Cloutsham.

The road is a quiet and secluded walk between woods that are the home of a sizeable population of deer. Cloutsham was originally a hunting lodge for the Acland family, three of whom were successively Wardens of Exmoor Forest from 1767 to 1814. Under their stewardship stag hunting revived on the moor as did the selective breeding of Exmoor ponies. In 1944 it was Sir Richard Acland who gave the Holnicote Estate to the National Trust, which includes some of the finest land on Exmoor. This was added to the land the Trust already owned on Dunkery Beacon.

Before Cloutsham the road bends sharp right and then after 400 metres left again. Follow it to where another road goes off on the right to Stoke Pero. On the left, opposite this junction, a bridleway leaves the road; follow this. It crosses a field diagonally to the right, cuts through the bottom corner of the next field and the top corner of the next. From here it swings left through the bottom corner of another field (stream on the left) and then out onto the moorland, going through a small conifer plantation. Follow it to the ridge ahead; Dunkery Beacon can be seen ahead and to the left. The bridleway crosses the track leading to Dunkery. Turn right and retrace your route back to the road.

Quantock hillforts and the Ridgeway

Dead Woman's Ditch – Robin Upright's Hill
Dowsborough hillfort – Ridgeway – Wilmot's Pool
Dead Woman's Ditch

A walk of just over 4 miles crossing the wild, upland country of the Quantocks. As well as exploring some of the Iron Age sites and ancient legends of this bracing hill country, there are magnificent views.

Time: Two hours.

Starting point: Parking place near Robin Upright's Hill, on the road from Crowcombe to Nether Stowey. The car park is at a junction where another road (which runs down to the Castle of Comfort pub, on the A39) leads off on the north side of the Crowcombe – Nether Stowey road. (Grid ref: 163 382).

Facilities: None but plenty at Nether Stowey, 2 miles distant. Also pub and village stores at Crowcombe, 1 mile away.

Problems: None.

Background: The Quantock Hills run 13 miles north-west to south-east. The northern part of the range is formed from rocks which produce a poor soil which, despite medieval attempts to cultivate it, has long since returned to heather and scrub oak. This has given the high ground a distinctly wild and bleak character, which contrasts with the oak woods in the valleys on its flanks. Farming has tended to concentrate on pasture for sheep and cattle and the cutting of timber and turf. Much of the upland is given over to stretches of commonland, covered by bracken and grass. Until the 13th century the Quantocks were royal forest. This does not mean that they were heavily wooded, rather that they were used for the hunting of deer.

Along the spine of the hills runs the prehistoric Ridgeway path with its Bronze Age round barrows, cairns and Iron Age hillforts and enclosures. These indicate that the hills – now deserted – were extensively used and visited in the distant past.

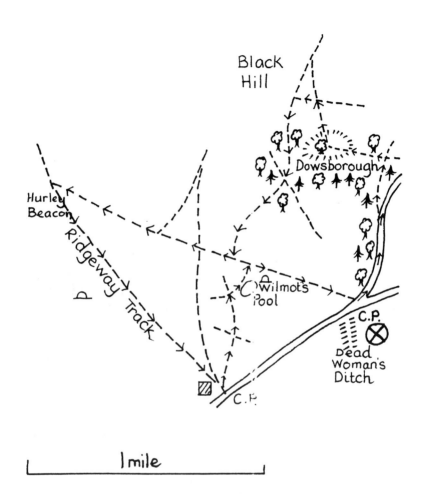

Black
Hill

Dowsborough

Hurley
Beacon

Ridgeway Track

Wilmots
Pool

C.P.

Dead
Woman's
Ditch

C.P.

|———————— 1 mile ————————|

Directions

To the left of the carpark and south of the road is a large bank and ditch.

This is called Dead Woman's Ditch and runs north-south on either side of the road to Crowcombe. It is an earth bank, up to 1.7 metres high, with a ditch on the west side and was probably some kind of boundary marker, connected with the Iron Age settlement in the hillfort at nearby Dowsborough. It was clearly not a defensive wall. It runs as far south as Rams Combe valley and as far north as Lady's Combe Valley.

It has been known by its present name since as least 1782. Ironically John Walford, a charcoal burner, murdered his wife, Jenny, nearby in 1789, and hid her body in the ditch. He was caught and hanged nearby.

From the carpark take the road opposite, signposted 'Dodington, Holford'. On the left side of this road are oak woods, with masses of bilberries in season. Follow the road downhill for a quarter of a mile, until the road bends right. 20 metres further on take the path off on the left. Follow this clear path, passing three paths joining it on the left. Your path goes uphill to a crossroads of paths on the brow of the hill. Turn left until at the top of the rise you cross the ramparts of a hillfort. The defensive ditch is clear on the left at this point.

This is Dowsborough, an Iron Age hillfort, which dates from somewhere between 700BC to the Roman invasion of AD43. Dowsborough is a simple hillfort, with only one surrounding bank and ditch, is oval in shape and encloses about 6 acres. In places the defensive bank, on which you are now standing, is still 4 metres above the outer ditch. The main entrance was on the eastern side and there was another in the northern defences.

Although the site is now deserted it would once have been home to a thriving community. The need for defence made higher areas like these very attractive for settlement in the past, and the nearby Ridgeway would have been a busy route. The fort is also called Danesborough. Local legends claim that it is haunted by a young Viking minstrel who, before being caught and killed, had fallen in love with a local girl. It is said his ghost still wanders the area around the fort, singing his sad laments. Other tales claim that at night the sounds of drunken laughter, or battle, echo from the fort.

Follow the track along the line of the ramparts. The interior of the fort is an oakwood, again seasonally carpeted with bilberries. On reaching a clearing, by a break in the ramparts on the right, look right.

To the north, the woods (to the right of the bare hill ahead) which run down to the (out of sight) A39, are called Shervage Wood. Legend claims they were terrorised by a dragon – the 'girt vurm of Shervage Wood' – until it was killed by a woodcutter from Stogumber.

Leave the hillfort by way of the first path down through the rampart. It leads down through moorland to a crossroads of paths. Turn left and follow the new path. (Ahead, across a valley, is the bulk of Black Hill.) After 150 metres, at a T-junction with another path, turn left. Follow this bridleway along the side of the hill into the oakwoods. A river valley is below to your right. The bridleway descends to a stream. Turn right, cross the stream, go up the bank and turn left along the path ahead. This path skirts the edge of Frog Hill on the right and passes through the oakwoods of Frog Combe and Lady Edge.

Local Quantock legends claim that oaks on the hills resent being cut and an oak coppice – above Butterfly Combe, near Holcombe – is meant to be haunted because its trees were once cut for coppicing.

Red deer can be seen in the woods, being introduced from Exmoor around 1860. Foxes and badgers are common and above the more open ground kestrels and buzzards hunt in some numbers.

Follow the path uphill. It eventually leaves the woods and goes out across the moor to meet a crossroad of tracks. Turn right and follow the line of the track westward. Near Hurley Beacon it joins the main Ridgeway route running along the spine of the hills. To get there the track is wide and clear. Go over one crossroads of tracks, pass another track joining from the right. Carry on to a T-junction with the main Ridgeway track at Hurley Beacon, by a fire-beater post.

On a clear day note the patchwork of different size fields in the vale ahead and far below you. This is an indication that many of them were created in the Middle Ages from the abundant pasture land in the area, when there were even attempts to plough parts of the Quantocks. However, attempts to grow even hardy crops like rye failed due to the poor soil. Until the 13th century the Quantocks were used for deer hunting, a leisure pursuit of royalty and the rich. The hills lay between two Anglo-Saxon royal estates at Cannington and Williton – useful bases for royal hunting parties.

Walkers on the Quantocks Ridgeway.

Looking down from the hills it is possible to see why the original British name of these uplands was 'Cantuc', meaning the 'rim', or 'circle'. To early settlers they seemed to be a barrier which divided the main area of what would one day be Somerset from the lands to the west.

At Hurley Beacon turn left onto the main Ridgeway.

Probably the most famous of English Ridgeways is that running from the Thames into Wiltshire, but the Quantock one reminds us that there are many of these old routeways that avoided wet, or wooded, low-lying areas and instead followed the line of the drier, high ground. The round barrows, cairns and other prehistoric sites dotted along, and near, this Ridgeway route indicate how important it once was. During the Middle Ages it was used as a drove road, to move livestock to and from the coast. It then became the main road between Taunton and the Bristol Channel and, as recently as the 19th century, was used to avoid waterlogged valley roads.

In the 1790s, this area of the central and northern Quantocks was a favourite place of the poets Samuel Taylor Coleridge and William Wordsworth, and Wordsworth's sister, Dorothy. The Wordsworths stayed at Alfoxton Park, 2 miles west of Holford, whilst Coleridge was then living in Nether Stowey. From there they explored the hills, often at night, and together worked on ideas that, in time, were to become some of the most famous poems in the English language. Local legends that the Ridgeway was haunted by supernatural dogs, called 'yeth hounds', may lie behind Coleridge's disturbing lines in *The Rhyme of the Ancient Mariner:*

> "Like one, that on a lonesome road
> Doth walk in fear and dread,
> And having once turned round walks on,
> And turns no more his head;
> Because he knows, a frightful fiend
> Doth close behind him tread."

Keep to the main track, ignoring any crossing tracks. Note the stone cairn on Hurley Beacon, just visible on the right as the Ridgeway crosses the brow of the hill. Walk on to a crossroad of tracks beside the blue gate of Crowcombe Park on the right. Walk ahead and towards the road. Just before the road turn left up another path, through bracken. Ignore the first crossing of paths, go on to the next cross of paths at the top of the hill and turn right. Stop by the pond, to the right of path.

This is Wilmot's, or Withyman's, Pool. Flint tools found here suggest that it was the site of a Stone Age seasonal hunter's camp, probably used in summer. The mound beyond the pool is a Bronze Age round barrow, whose hollow top indicates that it has been excavated in the past. Both remind us that the area was once settled, though it is now deserted.

Walk on, passing the pond on your right, to a crossroads with a larger track. You have been here before, after Dowsborough. Turn right. There are two tracks leading off, take the one to the left. Follow this for half a mile back to Dead Woman's Ditch car park.

Roman Lead Mining and a Mendip Roman Fort

Charterhouse – Rain's Batch – Velvet Bottom
Charterhouse

This walk of 3 ½ miles explores evidence of Roman life and industry in north-central Somerset, against the backdrop of striking Mendip scenery.

Time: Just under two hours

Starting Point: The walk starts and ends in the tiny Mendip settlement of Charterhouse, which lies on the unclassified road linking the B3134 and B3371, north-east of Cheddar. Park in the small lay-by near the church of St Hugh. (Grid ref: 502 557).

Facilities: There are no facilities at Charterhouse. The nearest are in Blagdon (2 ½ miles), or Cheddar (5 miles).

Problems: There are no problems. The walk is straightforward and undemanding.

Background: Charterhouse was the centre of the Roman lead mining industry on the Mendips. Excavations in the 19th century revealed not only a mining settlement but also a small fort and an amphitheatre. We even know the name of one of the Roman managers of the mine – Ascanius – as his name was stamped on one of the ingots, or pigs, of lead produced here.

Most of the Roman remains have been destroyed by later mining in the Middle Ages and 19th century, but Roman brooches, gems and implements have been found. The pock-marked land around Charterhouse – the 'gruffy grounds' – are evidence of medieval and later lead mining. The 'gruffs' are remains of the shafts which go down about 100 feet and were lined with dry-stone-walling. In the 13th century the Bishop of Wells was granted a royal license to use timber, from woods cleared near Cheddar, as pit props in one of the Charterhouse mines. Other veins of lead, closer to the surface, were dug out along shallow open-cast diggings, called 'grooves'.

The area around this settlement was part of the royal forest of Mendip in the Middle Ages. It was lightly forested and mostly

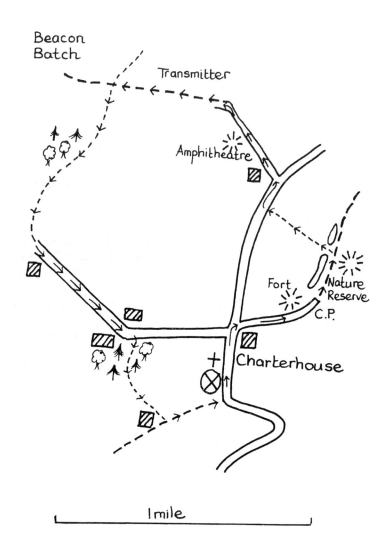

Beacon Batch

Transmitter

Amphitheatre

Nature
Reserve

Fort

C.P.

Charterhouse

1 mile

moorland. The old royal palace at Cheddar eventually passed from King John to the Bishop of Bath and Wells but John kept his hunting rights on Mendip. The monks who owned Charterhouse were frequently fined for poaching the king's deer (mostly red deer and some fallow).

Directions
Park beside the church.

Charterhouse is named from the Carthusian monks of Witham Priory, who were granted the right to work lead mines in the area by King Edward I in 1283. Mendip was later divided into four areas, or mining liberties, with their own laws but by 1795 many of these laws became obsolete when large areas of Mendip were enclosed.

With the church on your left walk forward, past the Charterhouse Education Centre on the right. At the crossroads immediately beyond, turn right. The narrow road comes to a dead-end near the entrance to a nature reserve.

From 1824 there was a revival of lead mining, based mostly on extracting lead from the 'slag' left by Roman and medieval miners and the disturbed areas ahead and to left and right are the remains of those later workings. Since 1970 the land in front has been a nature reserve of 70 acres. The lead mining poisoned the ground with a cocktail of chemicals but nature has fought back to reclaim the site and the reserve has two distinct types of rock under it (limestone and shale), giving it a split character. On the limestone are plants and animals that thrive on dry and rocky heathland, whilst on the shale there is wetland and coppiced woods. Amongst the more ususual plants found here is sea campion, normally a coastal flower, and there is a high adder and rabbit population. The reserve is also visited by rarer birds such as short and long-eared owls, redstarts, blackcaps and ever harriers.

Turn left and follow the track, going through the gate ahead. On the left below you, in the valley of Blackmoor, are the grassed over buddle pits and settling ponds used in Victorian lead extraction. Despite its wildness, this is an industrial landscape! Follow the path as it bends gently to the left. On the right is a patch of gorse and bracken. Go on to where a path crosses the track; it is waymarked. Stop and look back towards the church in the distance.

On the higher land, the other side of Blackmoor but before the trees, are the remains of a small Roman fort. It dates from shortly after the invasion of AD43 when Roman mining started. It was probably manned by a unit of soldiers from the II Legion Augusta, then stationed at Exeter. The fort site has been damaged in the past by ploughing and the mines probably spread north-east, east and south-east of it. Most of the Roman mines here were probably surface diggings worked by slave labour. The speed with which the entire operation was set up suggests that Roman military intelligence had identified the capture of Mendip mineral resources as one of the key objectives of their campaign in the West Country.

Go down the path which leaves the track here on the left. Notice the glassy lead slag on the ground. Cross the dam, with wet land on the right. Cross the footbridge and stile and go on to the road. Look diagonally left – between where you are standing and the trees is the site of the Roman civilian settlement.

The settlement was probably a small town but has not been extensively excavated. On aerial photographs it shows up as rectangular enclosures, platforms and sunken ways. The name of the settlement is uncertain. From the reign of Vespasian (AD69-79) the mines were leased to private companies, who extracted the 0.4% silver found in Mendip ore. Mendip lead was shipped as far as Pompeii, prior to its destruction following the eruption of Vesuvius in AD79.

Before you move on, look ahead to where, in the field opposite, are the remains of what was probably a medieval farmstead. The rectangular shape can be seen as a grassed over bank in the field. Then turn right and walk up the road.

The straight lines of the modern roads and hedges split up the landscape into rectangular blocks. This is the result of the 19th century enclosure of the open top of Mendip, before which the surrounding countryside would have had a much wilder and more exposed appearance.

After 60 metres take the road off on the left. It has 'No-Through Road' and 'Bridleway' signs. This is Rain's Batch. Pass a small clump of trees, before a bungalow, on the left. Walk on uphill. Pass an iron stile leading into a field on the right. A patch of gorse is noticable in this field, ahead and to your right.

The gorse grows over a small, rectangular earthwork, all that remains of another medieval settlement, surrounded by an earth embankment. It was probably a farmstead, with an entrance through the bank on the south-west corner. At the next hawthorn on the left, look into the field on the left where the circular

Lead mine workings, Charterhouse.

earthwork is all that remains of a Roman amphitheatre. The banks are still well preserved and rise 4.5 metres above the central floor of the arena, whilst there were entrances opposite one another on the east and west sides.

Carry on up the road to the TV masts. Turn left before the masts and follow a path, keeping the masts on your right. The path passes the masts and goes on between fields. There is dry stone wall on the left. The higher ground ahead is called Beacon Batch.

On Beacon Batch is a barrow cemetery consisting of ten round barrows, one of which was excavated by the Rev. John Skinner, of Camerton (see Walk 13) in 1820. On the other side of Beacon Batch (not included in this walk but easily accessible) are some long peat mounds which date from World War II. Originally constructed as decoys, they were supposed to look like the outlines of buildings when dim lights were lit at their ends. Decoy fires were also lit here to resemble a town on fire, with the aim of diverting German bombers from real targets.

Walk on gently downhill to where a footpath crosses the track, marked by yellow arrows. Turn left over a wooden stile and follow the ditch and stream, keeping them to your right. After about 800 metres cross a stile and pass a wood, in a deep cleft, on the right. Cross another stile. Ahead are two buildings by a road. Walk towards the right of the two and go over the stile in the corner of the field. Turn left and follow the quiet country road for about half a mile. After Manor Farm on the right the road bends to the left. On the bend, turn off right over an overgrown stone bridge, through trees, the path turns right, and up stone steps to a wooden stile. Walk on, bearing right, keeping the stone wall and farm on the right. Pass a very deep pothole, surrounded by a wall, on the right. Under no circumstances explore this open pothole. Pass slurry pit on left. Pass a wood on the right. Go over wooden stile beside a gate and walk on to the small building and the gravel track ahead.

The gravel track marks a routeway down Velvet Bottom which was probably used in Roman times to link the mines at Charterhouse with a villa at Cheddar. From here the River Yeo could be used to ship lead into the Bristol Channel.

Turn left up the gravel track. Note the 'gruffy' ground on the right. At the road, turn left and walk back up to the church at Charterhouse.

Priston Anglo-Saxon Estate

Stanton Prior – Wilmington – Priston Mill – Inglesbatch – Priston Tunley – Farmborough Common – Stanton Prior

A walk of 7 miles following the boundary of the Anglo-Saxon estate of Priston. The walk is an opportunity to compare the modern countryside with a detailed description of it written over a thousand years ago.

Time: Three and a half hours.

Starting Point: The walk starts and ends in Stanton Prior, southwest of Bath. (Grid ref: 678 627).

Facilities: Stanton Prior is a small farming hamlet and there are no facilities here. The closest are in Marksbury, 1 mile, with village facilities. Full facilities are in Keynsham, 4 miles.

Problems: No problems.

Background: This walk traces the boundary of an estate described in an Anglo-Saxon charter. Charters were written to clearly establish the area of an estate, describing any notable features of the landscape, ranging from rivers and large stones, to farms and shapes of fields. Reading a charter takes us back into the intimate details of life in the English countryside over a millenium ago.

The earliest charters date from the 670s, though most of the survivors, as with this one, date from the tenth century. The majority, like the one followed on this walk, record land given to the church and their descriptions of estate boundaries were in Old English. The Priston charter can be found printed, along with many others, in a 19th century collection called the *Cartularium Saxonicum*. The section giving the bounds runs to only 113 words, so is not a long document, and the oldest version of it exists in a 12th century copy.

The walk is through an attractive area of hill-country to the south of Stanton Prior, south of Bath. Much of it follows the boundary of the estate at Priston, which in AD931 was granted by the West Saxon King Athelstan to the abbey church of St Peter, in Bath.

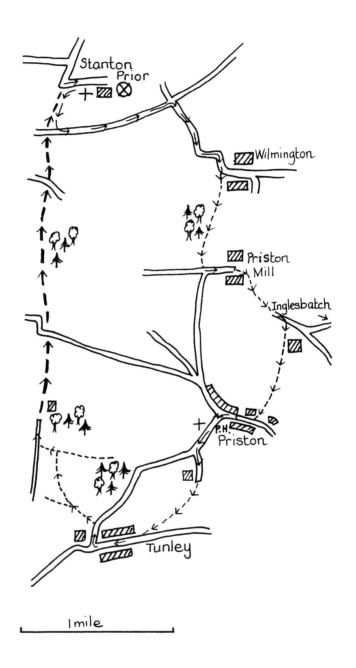

Stanton Prior

Wilmington

Priston Mill

Inglesbatch

Priston
P.H.

Tunley

1 mile

Directions

The walk starts in Stanton Prior. This can be reached by taking the A39 Bath-Marksbury road and turning off for Stanton Prior in the village of Marksbury. Park by Stanton Prior parish church.

Stanton Prior is a delightful hamlet whose long history is well represented by its parish church. Dating from at least 1297, the arms of Bath Abbey can still be seen carved into a wooden roof boss. Earlier Norman architecture survives in the walls. A holy water stoop (basin) can still be seen outside the main door and another is cut into the jamb of the door on the inside. Over the outside of the door an empty niche proclaims where a statue once stood. Bath Abbey owned the estate here throughout the Middle Ages.

Proceed out of the hamlet to the west. Church Farm is on your left. Immediately outside the hamlet the road bends sharply to the right. At this point turn left onto a rough track. Follow this track up the slope until it comes to a metalled road.

There is good reason for believing that this length of track is part of an ancient routeway which may be Roman, or even pre-Roman. It is one of a series of tracks running from the River Avon at Saltford to Camerton, where there was an important Roman and sub-Roman settlement. The track eventually joins the Roman Fosseway road north of Radstock and some modern archaeologists think it might have been used for the transport of salt, and call it the 'Salt Road'. The evidence for this is inconclusive but the name is still worth using to differentiate it from other tracks in the area. In the 10th century it formed the boundary between Anglo-Saxon estates at Marksbury, Stanton Prior and Priston.

On reaching the metalled road the Salt Road crosses it and continues south. However, at this point, leave it and turn left up the road. At once the road twists steeply up a hill. It soon becomes a hollow-way flanked by tall hedges.

This road is also ancient as in AD931 it marked the boundary between the estates of Stanton Prior and Priston, and still marks the parish boundary. It is mentioned in the Priston charter, where it is referred to as 'tha straet' (the street). In another charter, for an estate at nearby Marksbury, it is called the 'stanwei' (stoneway). Anglo-Saxon charters almost always proceed clockwise around an estate and we shall do the same.

Follow the road up to the summit of the hill and then along the plateau. To the left Stanton Prior nestles in the valley; behind it is Stantonbury hillfort. Behind you the view is clear to Dundry and the hillfort of Maes Knoll. Ahead Newton St Loe creeps up the hill in the middle distance. Follow the road until it comes to a crossroads. Turn right for Wilmington. For a little while you are leaving the boundary of the estate.

The crossroads you have left behind was called 'wynma dune' (Wynnmann's hill), from which Wilmington takes its name. Like most Anglo-Saxon landowners, whose names are recorded in modern place-names, we know nothing of Wynnmann but his name.

In Wilmington a wooden stile is set into a stone wall immediately after Stone Lea Cottage. Take this footpath south towards Priston Mill. Cross a small plot of land before coming to another stile. From here the path descends into a narrow valley. Keep the water trough on your left and make for the stile at the bottom of the field and cross the narrow brook. Climb the steep slope and then aim for the point at which a line of telephone poles meets the hedgeline. At the crest of the hill Wilmington Copse stretches away on your right. Cross a stile and head straight across the field to a gate. Follow the track down to the road. Turn left and Priston Mill is immediately on your right. Beyond the mill two footpaths leave the road, which finishes at this point. Take the one straight ahead and enter a field. Aim for the footbridge in the right hand corner of this field. It is at the junction of two streams (where the Conygre Brook joins the Newton Brook).

This area was called 'whitda combe' (white valley) in the time of Athelstan and the name survives in the field-name Whiddecombe. The eastern boundary of the Priston estate followed the course of the Newton Brook from east of Wilmington to where it rises at Westvale, near Nailwell.

After crossing the footbridge proceed for 20 metres and cross a stile on your right. Follow the line of telephone poles to the corner of the field and join a well defined farm track. Before you reach Home Farm a clearly marked stile on your right should be crossed. From this point white markers, on tree stumps, lead you down to another footbridge over the Newton Brook.

The place-name Ingelsbatch proclaims that this area was owned by an Anglo-Saxon named Ingel, who also owned land further to the north-east, remembered as Englishcombe ('Ingel's valley'). The word 'batch' comes from the Old English word 'bece' and here means a 'stream in a small valley'.

Cross the Newton Brook. At this point another stream joins it – the Priston Brook. Follow the path along the western bank of this new stream. You soon come to a coppice. Inside are the ruined remains of a cottage. The path skirts the wood and leads past a Wessex Waterboard installation to Priston, where it meets the metalled road by Village Farm.

The name Priston means the 'tun' (village) of the 'prysg' ('thicket'), suggesting that the narrow valleys in the area must have been fairly heavily wooded when the first Anglo-Saxon settlers arrived here.

Walk through the village. You will come to a fork in the road. To the right the road leads towards Marksbury and passes the church. You however take the left fork out of the village, called Priston Lane; Hill View is on your right. Follow the road down into the valley. At this point a road, on the left, leads to Rockhill House. Follow this road. Beyond the house it becomes a footpath, which leads up the hill to a gate. Instead of going through the gate, turn right, keeping the hedgerow on your left. This path turns into a bridleway which leads to the B3115 at Tunley. At the road turn right and proceed for half a mile.

You are now back on the boundary of the 934 charter, on a section of road it described as 'andlang herepathes west on thone thrylastan' (along the army-road, westward, to the stone with the hole in it). The stone was probably where Tunley Farm now is.

When you reach Tunley Farm take the lane on the right which leads back towards Priston. It is not signposted but the junction is on the brow of a hill. After 100 metres on this side-road turn left over a stile, straight after a metal field-gate. This footpath passes to the east of a small Iron Age fort. Follow the hedgeline, keeping it on your left, until the hedge bends sharply left and then right. In this corner is another stile. Ignore this and keep following the hedgeline.

Curiously, those who drew up the charter also skirted the fort and in the 10th century the place where the modern hedge kinks was then the site of the 'haran stone' (the hoar stone). This literally means 'the lichen covered stone', a term used for an old stone boundary marker, which alas stands there no longer.

After the kink in the hedge, follow the path downhill. On the right is Priston Wood. Coming to an iron gate, there is a smaller clump of trees on your left. The path follows the eastern edge of this smaller block of trees. Stop at the gate.

You have reached one of the most intriguing points on the charter, called the 'ealdan sele', meaning the 'old hall'. In the 8th century poem *Beowulf* the phrase: 'The hall towered high, lofty and wide gabled' was written 'Sele hlifade heah ond horn geap'. Near where you are standing was the site of such a building. Even in the 10th century it was called old!

Go through the gate and downhill until you reach the stream. You are on its south bank. This stream was named the 'Lox': an unknown name, in the language spoken before the Anglo-Saxons settled here. At the stream turn left and walk along its bank. Follow the stream until it leads to another metalled road.

As you walk beside the stream look right across the water. This was the site of 'Leomannes graf' (Leofman's grove). A narrow stretch of woodland now occupies the shoulder of the hill. (There is a possibility that it may have meant Leofman's grave.)

When you reach the road you are once more back on the ancient route which formed the western boundary of the Priston estate. Turn right and follow the road until it ends at Lammas Field Cottage. On your right a track leads to Lammas Field Farm. At the cottage cross the stile on your left, turn right and follow the hedge, keeping it on your right. You reach a gateway leading into another field. Go through it, passing an old sheep dip on your left. The route passes a striking knoll on the left. Keep following the hedge on your right.

As you pass the knoll the hedgebank becomes higher and wider. Soon the ditch beside it becomes a distinct hollow-way, or sunken road. This was called the 'ealdan dic' (the old ditch/dyke).

Entering another field, via a gate, the bank and ditch dies away. As you approach the large knoll of Priest Barrow on your right, a stile takes you onto the eastern side of the hedgerow. Follow this, past Priest Barrow, until you arrive at a metalled road. You reach the road at a point where it kinks right and then left again. Halfway through the kink a gateway on your right allows you into a field. Go through it and, keeping the hedge on your left, proceed. After 250 metres you drop down to the Conygre Brook.

The kink in the road is where a track from Priston met the Salt Road. It followed the route of this more important track for a bare 50 metres then cut off westward continuing on its way to Farmborough. As you reach the Conygre Brook you are at 'readan ford' (red ford). Just before you reach the brook, notice how the colour of the soil about you changes. The old description survives in the modern field-name Redfield.

Cross the Conygre Brook, using the stepping stones. Follow the path uphill. On the right you can see a patch of woodland across a field. Beyond it is Priston New Farm. As you reach the top of the slope the gradient levels out until you reach another metalled road.

Before you reach the road, see how the hedgebank and ditch grows in size once more. It is a survival of the same 'old ditch' that you last saw on Farmborough Common.

Cross the road and ahead of you the Salt Road survives as a clearly defined track between hedgerows. Follow this track for a short distance to the next metalled road. You have now completed the circuit of this walk. Ahead of you, over the road, is the trackway that you followed earlier to this point, from Stanton Prior. Follow this again, in the opposite direction. It will lead you back to Stanton Prior.

Stanton Prior

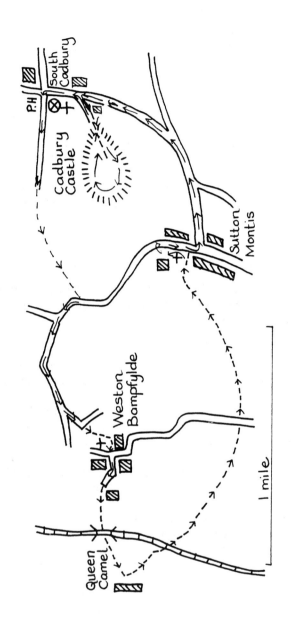

P.H

South
Cadbury

Cadbury
Castle

Sutton
Montis

Weston
Bompfylde

Queen
Camel

1 mile

King Arthur Country

South Cadbury – Cadbury Castle hillfort – Weston Bampfylde
Queen Camel – Sutton Montis – South Cadbury

This walk of 6 miles is through a countryside overshadowed by the legendary exploits of the Dark Age King Arthur. It includes a fascinating hillfort, of national importance, and attractive villages set in a little explored area of south eastern Somerset. All 6 miles can be walked, or the hillfort section can be separated and regarded as a shorter walk.

Time: Three hours for the whole walk.

Starting Point: The village of South Cadbury. (Grid ref: 632 255)

Facilities: There is a pub in South Cadbury, the Red Lion, but no other facilities. The closest facilities are in Queen Camel, 3 miles. Yeovil, Wincanton and Castle Cary are all fairly close.

Problems: The walk is straightforward and undemanding.

Background: The walk offers a mix of upland scenery at Cadbury Castle, with pleasant pastures along the banks of the Somerset Cam and some attractive smaller villages.

A number of legends associate King Arthur with the area surrounding this striking hillfort. Whether there is any historical reality behind this is open to question, but archaeologists have revealed that the hillfort was an impressive stronghold for a powerful local chieftain in the years following the end of Roman rule. This does not prove that the chieftain was Arthur, but it does suggest a grain of truth in the legends.

Perhaps you will experience the atmosphere of the place, as John Steinbeck experienced it in 1959, on a day that was 'noble gold . . . mystic, wonderful', but determined to 'go back over and over . . . at night and in the rain.' It is indeed a place of many moods.

Directions

Park in the small lay-by beside the parish church in South Cadbury. The reference to the group of churches known as the 'Camelot Parishes' on the notice board is an unexpected reminder of the legends we have come to enjoy.

South Cadbury takes its name from the hillfort to its south west. The name is Old English and means Cada's 'burg', or 'fort'. Although the village is now small, its eastern end was once a separate settlement, named Littleton, and the name survives in that of a field-name.

Beyond the church – on the edge of the village – a track leads up to Cadbury Castle from the Sutton Montis road. It is signposted 'Castle Lane leading to Camelot Fort'. This name for the hillfort is a modern invention. Go up the track.

The track leading from South Cadbury church to the hillfort is called Arthur's Lane, a name of uncertain provenance. In 1542 the Tudor historian Leland visited the area and wrote: 'At the very south end of the chirch of South Cadbyri standith Camallate, sumetyme a famose toun or castelle. The people can telle nothing ther but that they have hard say Arture much resortid to Camalat.' This mention is the earliest link between Arthur and the area and is possibly an invention of Leland. When the 18th century antiquarian Stukeley visited the hillfort in 1723 he found 'the country people are ignorant of this name [Camalat]', but only knew the place as Cadbury Castle. Camelot itself, as Arthur's court, was an invention of 12th century writers of Arthurian romance and had no geographical location in their stories.

Follow the track up through the woods, which in spring are awash with bluebells and primroses. You pass though a gate with a wooden stile, and beyond it the earth ramparts rise on either side of the track. About halfway between the gate and the ridge a muddy cattle path goes off on the left along the base of one of the ramparts. It leads to a metal cattle trough. Go up the track a few metres to where, tucked into the side of the bank on your right, is the stone and brick top of a blocked well, now called Arthur's Well.

The connection between Arthur and Cadbury has created a rich body of legends, one of which has his hounds drinking here on stormy winter nights, before following their ghostly master out along Arthur's Hunting Causeway, an old track leading away from the fort. Another states that anyone pure in heart, who washes their eyes at the Well on Midsummer Eve, will see the hill open and Arthur and his knights asleep inside.

Go back to the main track and walk up into the hillfort. This entrance, on the north-eastern side of Cadbury Castle, is one of three such gateways. Walk clockwise around the fort ramparts.

Cadbury Castle hillfort.

Cadbury Castle is not of course a 'castle'. It is an Iron Age hillfort, built on an isolated hill made of limestone and sandstone. Excavations show that it was first occupied about 3300BC. The hill was again settled in the Late Bronze Age, though the striking Iron Age ramparts and ditches were added from about 500BC. They enclose over 17 acres and its four massive earth banks were altered several times. The ramparts themselves are very impressive. Leland remarked: 'What daungerous steepenesse . . . it is a mirackle, both in arte and nature.'

Walk on towards the first gap in the bank and cross it – the fort's eastern gate. The view east (left) is cut off by the hills; the view south (ahead) extends towards the Dorset Downs; the view westward is excellent and Glastonbury Tor can be seen on a clear day. Continue following the ramparts, Sutton Montis village and church can be seen below. Walk on to the next break in the ramparts.

This is the site of the south-western gate, which was burnt down in about AD70, during a Roman attack on the fort. In the later Roman period there was probably a pagan temple on the hill.

Go down into the gateway.

Between AD400 and 600 the fort was reoccupied. So little is known about this shadowy period between the end of Roman rule and the arrival of the Anglo-Saxons it is called the Dark Ages. However scant the evidence, we can be sure that whoever refortified this hillfort was a powerful local chieftain. An impressive timber gatehouse, along with refurbished ramparts and a timber breastwork made the hill into a fortress once more.

The walling that can be seen here (and elsewhere around the perimeter) dates from the later 18th, or 19th century. It was probably built in order to allow cattle to graze the banks without damaging the crops grown on the top of the hill.

Looking back into the interior of the fort, there is a knoll of higher ground ahead. Walk to this.

After the 7th century, settlement on the hill ceased, only beginning again in the late Anglo-Saxon period. The hill then became a small fortified town (called Cadanbyrig), during the reign of King Ethelred, probably as a refuge from Viking attacks. Coins were minted and a stone wall built around the top of the hill. With the end of Viking raids the settlement was abandoned early in the 11th century.

Climb up to the top of the higher ground.

The highest part of the plateau here has been identified as Arthur's Palace since the 1580s, when William Camden mockingly mentioned it in his book, *Britannia*. This name was probably inspired by Leland's writing, 40 years earlier. More intriguingly, the excavations on the summit in the 1960s revealed that a Dark Age timber hall had once stood here. Pottery finds suggest that wine and other luxury goods were arriving from the Mediterranean and nearby were the foundations of a church dating from the later Anglo-Saxon use of the site.

Looking south-westward, down the slope that you have climbed, notice how the sides of the knoll have slumped in places, making depressions in the hillside.

According to legends, first recorded in the 16th century, the hill is hollow, with Arthur inside. It is said that a local man asked a 19th century historian investigating the site, 'Have you come to awaken the king?'

Complete the circuit of the ramparts; then go back down the track to South Cadbury village. Walk back past the church and turn left before the Red Lion, into Folly Lane. This turns into a wide track, which leads into a field. Walk straight on, keeping the hedge on your right. Ignore a stile on your right and carry on until a gateway on the right leads onto a country road. Turn right and follow the road. Ignore a road joining from the right. Pass two houses on the right.

The road bends right and on the left is an ornamental gateway. Turn left down this drive. After 100 metres the drive bears left, on the right is a metal kissing-gate. Go through and walk to the church, through two metal gates and a wooden one.

You have reached the hamlet of Weston Bampfylde, which in the early 13th century was owned by Richard Baumfilde – hence its name. The church was described by Collinson in 1791 as a 'plain single building', but actually it has an attractive octagonal tower and an interesting modern statue of a woman with a flying bird in the graveyard. The bell clappers, from 1450, now hang on the inside wall of the tower.

Leave the churchyard through the white gate. On reaching the road go straight across. Notice the hand-pump in the field behind you. Follow the narrow road past stone-built Field House on your left. A short track leads to a gate. Stop here and look down into the slight valley of the River Cam.

This stream takes its name from the nearby village-name of Queen Camel. However, Arthurian interest in the area has encouraged some to imaginatively suggest that it is Camlann, where Arthur met his tragic death in early Welsh tradition. Despite local stories of farmers ploughing up evidence of a terrible battle, there is no record of a mass grave here and the closest Dark Age burials have been found in an Anglo-Saxon cemetery (containing no more than three burials) north of Queen Camel, on Camel Hill.

Go through the gate and bear left to the stile near the top corner of the field. Cross it and walk to where the path goes under the bridge of the railway ahead. (Cross another stile and gate to reach the bridge.) Framed in the arch of the bridge is the tower of the parish church of Queen Camel.

Queen Camel takes its name from the Welsh words for the hill to the north-west, 'cant' (rim, or ridge) and 'moel' (bare) and from Queen Eleanor, who was given the manor in 1275 by her husband, Edward I. Leland claimed that the second part of the name was really 'Camallat', clearly a piece of wishful thinking, to support his identification of South Cadbury as Arthur's capital, Camelot.

Go under the railway and through the left of the two metal gates. Walk towards the oak tree in the hedge ahead. To the left of the tree is a gap in the hedge and a stile beyond. Cross the stile and turn left (to the right is a view of the church). Walk to the stile ahead. Cross a wooden, then a stone stile, marked with the sign of the Leland Trail.

Cross the field to the next stile. Cross this stile and railway (with great care) to another stile. Cross it and keep the hedge on your left. Cross two close-set stiles. After the second stile walk ahead, keeping the large oak tree to your left. Cross the next stile and walk diagonally right to the trees in the far corner of the field. Cross the stile, plank bridge and stile. Walk to the next stile, a stream on your right. At the road turn right and then left back into a field. Keep the trees to the left and walk on along the edge of the field. At the end of the field, aim for a stile in the right hand corner. Cross it and walk towards Sutton Montis church. Cross the stile in the right hand corner of the field, then the next stile ahead and go up to the churchyard.

It is claimed that Sutton Montis is haunted by Arthur and his knights, who water their horses here after riding down from the hill above. The well in question lies in the grounds of Abbey House, a 15th century priest's house, near the church.

To see Abbey House, go out of the churchyard, turn left down the hill and just around the bend it is on the left. The well, which is on private property, is in the orchard to the left of the house. Go back up the hill, passing the church and at the edge of the village, take the road on the left signposted 'South Cadbury 1 mile'. After about half a mile the road bends left around the eastern flank of the hillfort. Just before this point there is a footpath off on the right, signposted 'Sigwells' and a road – Crangs Lane – joins on the right. You carry on along the road to South Cadbury.

A number of books talk of a trackway, called Arthur's Hunting Causeway, running from Cadbury to Glastonbury and supposedly haunted by the king and his warriors. They are remarkably vague about where this track runs. In fact there is no ancient track running towards Glastonbury. The only old routeway near the hillfort is one which runs from Sherborne to Shepton Mallet and this road is part of it. However, north of here this route does cross Arthur's Bridge, near Ditcheat, and it was probably this which inspired the whole Hunting Causeway legend and the destination of Glastonbury was added because it claims to be Arthur's burial place.

Return to the church at South Cadbury.

King Alfred and Athelney

*Athelney – Burrowbridge – Stoke St Gregory
East Lyng – Athelney*

This walk of 7½ miles visits a site famed in English history and explores the Somerset moors around it.

Time: Four hours.

Starting Point: Athelney. (Grid ref: 346 291).

Facilities: Small village facilities at Stoke St Gregory. More facilities at Othery, 2 ½ miles. Full facilities at Taunton, 7 ½ miles.

Problems: The walk contains a mix of lane, drove and footpaths due to the limited rights of way in the vicinity of Athelney, creating some short linear sections in an otherwise circular walk.

Background: The events the walk celebrates surround that most famous of all Anglo-Saxon kings, Alfred of Wessex – the only king in English history to be surnamed 'the Great' by later historians. The story is set in the year 878, when Wessex was at the mercy of Danish Viking invaders and Alfred was fighting to preserve both his kingdom and his life. Already these marauders from Scandanavia had crushed the English kingdoms of Northumbria, East Anglia and Mercia. In two of these kingdoms the rulers had been ritually tortured to death. Now it seemed it was the turn of the English of southern and western England – the West Saxons.

Shortly after twelfth night, in early January 878, a Viking army led by Guthrum mounted a lightning raid on Wessex. Striking from Gloucester, where they had been wintering, they seized the royal residence at Chippenham and forced Alfred into a headlong retreat into the Somerset marshes. To many West Saxons it looked as if Alfred was doomed and the *Anglo-Saxon Chronicle* records that many of his subjects submitted to the invaders. Yet in the wetlands of Somerset the king, accompanied by a small number of loyal followers, was defiantly preparing a last ditch effort to expel the Vikings. This counter-attack was planned from the king's base at Athelney.

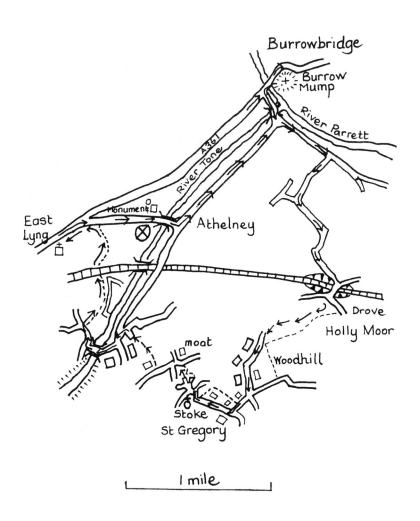

Burrowbridge

Burrow Mump

River Parrett

A361

River Tone

Monument

East Lyng

Athelney

Drove

Holly Moor

moat

Woodhill

Stoke St Gregory

1 mile

Athelney Farm, with the monument just visible between the farmhouse and the barn on the right-hand side.

Directions
Park at Athelney near the bridge over the River Tone.

The name of Athelney means 'the island of the princes' and it is likely that Alfred was long familiar with it as a royal hunting base. It is also possible that there was a small religious community here, perhaps a hermitage. Perhaps most importantly, its isolated position deep in the marshes provided Alfred and his followers with a defensive refuge from which to launch an attack.

The site is actually comprised of two low hills – now behind and west of Athelney Farm – raised up from the surrounding moors and commanding the junction of the Rivers Parrett and Tone. In Alfred's day the whole area would have been a wilderness of creeks and pools subject to heavy flooding in winter. Later drainage has dramatically changed the landscape and the course of the River Tone was diverted in the Middle Ages.

The *Anglo-Saxon Chronicle* records that around Easter 878 Alfred built a stronghold here and began to rally the West Saxons to his cause. His biographer and contemporary – Asser, Bishop of Sherborne – adds that from this base the king began to harry the Vikings. The fort at Athelney probably consisted of little more than a ditch, bank and palisade, and in the mid tenth century was still known as the 'eald herworth' (old army enclosure).

According to a 10th century life of St Neot, written in eastern England, it was at Athelney that Alfred allowed loaves to burn while sheltering incognito in the hut of a swineherd and his wife; his mind being distracted with more pressing thoughts. In the 16th century this story was added to the first printed edition of Asser's *Life of King Alfred*, and has become the most famous story of all the legends with which he is associated.

Whatever the truth, the king turned probable defeat into victory. In the seventh week after Easter, he left his base and rode east to the Somerset-Wiltshire border where his agents had assembled an army. Two days later they defeated the Vikings at Edington (Wiltshire) and went on to besiege them for 14 days at Chippenham and force their complete surrender – a remarkable turn-around in Alfred's fortune.

At the main unsignposted entrance of Athelney Farm (which lies further up the minor road to East Lyng) turn into the drive and follow it to the rear of the farmhouse. Climb up the steps and at the top there is a view of the Athelney Abbey commemorative monument. This is not a public right of way but the landowner has kindly given permission to view the monument.

King Alfred's Monument, Athelney.

In about 888 – according to Asser – Alfred founded an abbey here. The choice of site clearly indicated the king's gratitude to God for his deliverance from the Vikings and was also part of his campaign to revive learning in a country ravaged by war.

The abbey may have been destroyed in later Viking raids and there is evidence to suggest it was refounded in 960. The abbey was not wealthy and by the time it was dissolved in 1539 was heavily in debt. Nothing of it survives above ground and even its foundations were dug out in 1674. The monument dates from 1801 (remarkably surveys conducted in 1993 reveales that it stands exactly over the crossing of the abbey church).

Retrace your steps to the road. Turn left, follow the road and cross the River Tone. Turn left at the road junction, signposted 'Burrowbridge, Bridgwater'. Follow the road for three quarters of a mile. At a T-junction turn left, cross the River Tone again and go on to another T-junction with the A361 and turn right. This is Burrowbridge.

This bridge used to be the only crossing of the River Parrett between Bridgwater and Langport. Built in 1826, it was a toll bridge until 1945.

Cross the bridge and go on to the entrance gate to Burrow Mump on the right. Climb up to the church.

Burrow Mump is a sandstone hill which, until the drainage of the surrounding moors, was frequently made an island by flooding. It is in a strong strategic position, being sited at the confluence of the River Tone (and the old course of the River Cary) with the Parrett. Tradition has it that this is the site of 'King Alfred's Fort', although there is, as yet, no archaeological evidence to support the claim. However, there may have been a fortification here in the 12th century and there has been a church on the site since the early 13th century, when it was called 'St Michael of la Burghe'.

The church – dedicated to St Michael – was ruinous in 1645 when Royalist troops sought refuge here after their defeat at the battle of Langport. A new chapel was begun at the end of the 18th century but was not completed. The hill commands extensive views and is so close to Alfred's forts at Athelney and Lyng that it may have been used as a lookout point.

From the top of the hill there are fine views over Southlake Moor. One of the lowest lying of the Somerset wetlands, it belonged to Glastonbury Abbey in the Middle Ages, who were responsible for draining it. In about 1255 three walls were built around it to keep

Barrow Mump and the junction of the rivers Tone and Parrett at dusk.

out the River Parrett. One, named Burrow Wall, ran from Burrow Mump to Othery and is still followed by the A361; a second, South-lake Wall, can still be seen running along the bank of the Parrett; a third, Challis Wall, protected the moor on its eastern side.

The area received further protection from winter floods when the River Carey was diverted in 1791 through King's Sedgemoor.

From the 19th century controlled flooding, or 'warping', was practiced in order to fertilise the land with silt and the moor is now rich in many breeds of wildfowl when in flood.

Retrace your steps to Burrowbridge. Turn left after the Parrett Bridge and follow the road. Pass the road you walked down earlier joining on your right. Walk straight on down the new road, signposted 'Stathe, Langport'. After about 800 metres you pass a pumping station on the right. Pass Withy Orchard on the left – the housename fixed to the wheel of an old horse-rake. After 100 metres a drove leaves the road on the right, immediately before The Old King William house and opposite the wall embanking the Parrett. Go down this drove. After half a mile and after withy beds on the left, you reach a T-junction with another drove. Turn left and follow the new drove. After 600 metres it kinks right and after 200 metres kinks right and then left, to a junction with a metalled road where a railway line goes under the road in a cutting.

Turn right, cross over the railway and turn left onto another drove before Bullplace Farm. Follow this for 400 metres. A footpath leaves the drove on the right at a point where the left side of the drove ceases to be fenced. Go through the second of the gates on your right and walk ahead keeping the hedge on your right. Go towards an old gate set in the hedge ahead. Cross it and follow the hedge on your right.

Pass a gate on your right and cross an overgrown gate in the corner of the field ahead. Walk diagonally left across the field to a gate in the corner by a tree and circular water trough. Go into the lane and turn right, walking on to where the lane bends sharply right. Go straight on over the wooden stile ahead (high bank on your right), to cross another stile. Keep the hedge on your left and cross another stile. Aim for the gap in the corner of the hedge ahead and go on to cross the next stile and turn into the road. This is Stoke St Gregory.

Turn left and follow the road. Pass the Rose and Crown pub (an excellent resting place) and keep following the road which eventually swings round to the church on your left.

The church at Stoke St Gregory, with its attractive octagonal tower, dates mostly from the 14th century and contains some interesting monuments and a carved wooden pulpit.

A custom called Egg Shackling occurs at the village school on Shrove Tuesday in which eggs marked by the children are shaken in a sieve, the last remaining uncracked egg being the winner.

Return to the road and walk down to where the village stores are on your left. Turn right, then left into Church Close. A cul de sac leads off on the right, at the end follow the path on the left which leads to a stile. Cross it and keep the hedge on your right until you reach a road. Go over the stile.

Slough Court farm lies in front of you. It is late medieval and defended by a moat; its gateway dates from the 16th century.

Turn left and follow the road to the end of Slough Lane. Go over a wooden stile on the right, immediately before a thatched cottage. Aim for another stile ahead and go over it, passing a white cottage on your right. Cross another stile and then a gate and aim for the gate ahead, by the power lines. Go into the next field and then through the gate on the left side. Pass a brick-built long cottage on your right and go on to the metal gate ahead which leads onto a track. Follow the track a short distance to a lane and turn left, passing houses and a withy working showroom on the left, to reach a metalled road. This is an area called Curload. At the road turn left and then right into a lane, marked 'public footpath'. Follow the lane which bears right to reach the bank of the River Tone. Bear left and cross the river via a metal bridge.

Turn right and then immediately left down a drove which leads away from the river. Go over a small bridge which crosses a drainage rhyne. Immediately after the bridge turn right off the drove onto a path and follow the drainage rhyne, keeping it on your right. After a small building on the right you reach Crooked Drove and turn left. This drove crosses a bridge over a larger drainage channel and eventually turns sharp right before the railway line. You go on and cross the line (take great care). Walk on through three fields following the hedgeline on your right. This eventually leads to a metalled road by a small building. At the road turn left and follow it towards East Lyng.

This road goes from Athelney to East Lyng, the location of a second fortress built after that at Athelney and linked to it by a narrow causeway. This lane follows the line of a 12th century drainage rhyne, which itself probably followed the line of the ninth century causeway, which, according to Bishop Asser, took 'protracted labour' to build. The major obstacle it faced was a river which once flowed between Athelney and Lyng. This suggests that the causeway was, in fact, a fortified bridge protecting the eastern approach to Lyng.

At the junction with the A361 turn left and follow the road to East Lyng. At the church go to the rear wall of the grave yard with a view into the field beyond.

The defences at Lyng consisted of a large bank and ditch protecting the promontory from attack from the west and traces of these defences survive in this field. Asser described the fort as 'a formidable fortress of elegant workmanship'. Alfred established a series of these defended 'burhs' across Wessex to provide refuge from Viking attack and royal military and trading bases. The other burhs in Somerset were Axbridge, Bath, Langport and Watchet.

The church is worth a visit as it is famous for its richly decorated bench-ends. Dating from the 16th and 17th centuries they include carvings of a Green Man, a pelican, a monkey riding backwards on a beast, a miller carrying sacks of corn and many others.

Return to Athelney.

Another place of interest
After the walk it is worth driving across to Aller, which was the site of the church in which the Viking King Guthrum was baptised, as part of the Treaty of Wedmore which followed Alfred's victory at Edington. Alfred's decision to include this as part of the peace arrangements reveals his desire to build a lasting settlement between Wessex and its enemies, based on a common faith. Guthrum came here with thirty of his leading followers three weeks after Alfred's triumph, after which he was entertained by Alfred at the king's estate at Wedmore.

The present church at Aller dates from the 12th and 13th centuries and so the font is not the one in which Guthrum was baptised. Nevertheless it was probably on this spot that his baptism took place.

The Alfred Jewel, found only 4 miles from Athelney, and inscribed 'Alfred ordered me to be made'.

Norman Power and a Medieval New-Town

Montacute – St Michael's Hill and castle site – Montacute

This short 2 mile walk explores one of Somerset's most attractive villages.

Time: 1½ hours.

Starting point: The Market Place, called The Borough. (Grid ref: 498 169).

Facilities: A small selection of pubs, restaurants, tea-shops, Post Office, small shops.

Problems: A steep climb up St Michael's Hill, which can be made much easier by using an alternative route. There is also an optional climb up the tower on St Michael's Hill.

Background: Montacute is famous for the beautiful golden stone of its buildings, which was quarried from nearby Ham Hill. The castle was built by 1068, making it one of the earliest Norman castles in Somerset, though it and its lands soon passed to the priory founded here in 1102. The priory developed the manor as a 'new town' and this has shaped its lay-out to the present day.

By 1306 it was large enough to send two members to parliament. By the 16th century it had a Guildhall, many shops and a butchers area (a 'shambles'). In the 18th and 19th centuries it was a glove making centre.

Directions
Park in the market place by the fountain errected in 1902 to celebrate the coronation of King Edward VII.

The walk through this splendid village starts in the open market place. There was a settlement near here before the priory was founded, probably in the part now called Bishopston. The area around the market place was built by the monks after 1102 and designed to boost their income by enlarging the existing settlement. As well as adding to their rent roll, they benefited from the trade at the new market. The new development became known as The Borough.

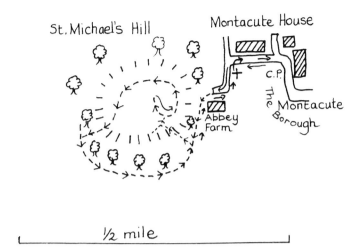

St. Michael's Hill

Montacute House

C.P.

The Montacute Borough

Abbey Farm

½ mile

The main street from the Borough, Montacute.

Montacute House.

The buildings around it have the narrow fronts and long, narrow back gardens common to medieval town buildings, called 'burgage plots'. The fronts of most of the houses here today date from the 18th and 19th centuries, but they are rebuildings of much older properties. An interesting example stands on the south side of the square, called The Milk House Licensed Restaurant. It has an ancient plank door with strap hinges.

Walk towards the entrance of Montacute House.

From the corner of The Borough the drive leads into Montacute House, the Elizabethan mansion, built between 1590-99, for Sir Edward Phelips. Sir Edward's great uncle had been a minor tenant of the priory but by 1604, Sir Edward himself had become Speaker of the House of Commons and Master of The Rolls. And his house had replaced the priory as the great landowner at Montacute in just over half a century!

The house has been owned by the National Trust since 1931 and now contains an excellent collection of Tudor and Stuart paintings from the National Portrait Gallery. They are housed in a Long Gallery on the second floor, which is the longest room of its type in the country.

Standing by the iron gates, at the entrance to the house, the handsome building on your right is Montacute Cottage, which dates from about 1500.

The house built on the end of Montacute Cottage and facing the main road is 16th century and is named The Chantry. It was the home of Robert Sherborne, the last prior of Montacute and his initials can be seen carved in the panel below the upstairs window.

Leave The Borough, walking down Middle Street.

Middle Street was known as Bowtell Street in 1551. To the right is the area still called Bishopston, the focus of the original settlement. The King's Arms stands on the edge of the original village.

On your left is the church. Go inside through a door decorated with fine wrought-iron work.

The parish church of St Catherine has some fine Norman stonework (eg. the chancel arch). It was largely rebuilt by the monks, in about 1170-80. The rest of the chancel, transepts and north porch date from a later building phase and the tower was erected in the early 16th century. The north transept contains monuments to the Phelips family, whose fine effigies, dating from 1484-1598, give an insight into changing fashions. The Powys family have strong connections with this church, as the father of the trio of literary sons was vicar here between 1885 and 1914. The West Country features in a number of the novels written by his sons, most notably John Cowper Powys's *A Glastonbury Romance* (1932), *Weymouth Sands* (1934) and Llewelyn Powys's *Somerset Essays* (1937).

Return outside.

The south face of the tower is deliberately without decoration as it once was a fives court. On the south side of the church, by a yew tree, is the remains of a medieval cross (possibly 15th century), which once stood at the front of the church. The carvings on it are badly weathered but one has been identified as Reginaldus Cancellarius, a 12th century benefactor of the priory.

Go and look over the wall on the south side of the graveyard.

The large field beyond the graveyard was the site of the priory. All that survives is a square dovecote, some earthworks and the remains of the monastic fishpond.

Go back to the main entrance to the churchyard. Turn left and immediately left again. It is signed 'No Through Road'. Pass Montacute National School, built in 1847, on the right.

Ahead is the mainly sixteenth century gatehouse of Montacute

An 18th century engraving of St. Michael's Hill and Montacute House.

Priory, now Abbey Farm, which has an attractive window over the entrance. The Cluniac priory of Saints Peter and Paul was founded by William de Mortain, who endowed it with the borough of Montacute, the castle and the manor of Bishopston. He did so as an alternative to facing a charge of conspiring against the Crown.

In 1539 the priory was dissolved on the orders of Henry VIII, the monastery church was demolished and the other buildings sold. Later, when Montacute House was built, the lands, including Abbey Farm became part of the Phelips estate.

Take the footpath right, signposted 'Hedgecock Hill Wood'. Cross the yard in front of the abbey gatehouse to the track beyond. Look up the wooded slope.

The hill is owned by the National Trust and the town takes its name from it. First recorded in 1086 as 'Montagud', it means 'Pointed Hill' and the Latin form of this – 'Mons acutus' – gave rise to Montacute. Before The Borough was built, the monks held fairs on the hill.

Walk up the sunken track between the trees.

A medieval manuscript, called 'De Inventione Sancte Crucis', records the discovery, in 1035 during the reign of King Cnut, of a miraculous cross on the summit of the hill. According to legend the holy relic – a fragment of the True Cross – was taken to his Essex estate by Tofi, a Saxon landowner in both Somerset and Essex, who built Waltham Abbey to house it. After Tofi's death, the cross was owned by King Harold Godwinson, killed at the Battle of Hastings and buried at Waltham Abbey.

Follow the path left around the base of the hill. Where it forks, take the right path upwards. The wood is on your right. You come to a stile on your right. Go over it into the wood and ascend the steep slope. [For those wishing to avoid the climb, do not go into the wood. Instead, follow the base of the hill keeping the fence on your right. You come to another stile on your right, with a National Trust sign. Go over it and follow the gravel path to the summit.]

After the Norman Conquest, Robert Count of Mortain built a castle on the holy hill, an act of sacrilege which led to a revolt by the Saxons of Somerset and Dorset in 1068. This uprising against Norman rule coincided with a landing in Somerset by the sons of Harold and may have been organised by them. However, the revolt failed and the Saxon siege of Robert's new castle was broken by the Bishop of Coutances, who was another Norman landholder in Somerset.

Near the top of the steep slope you meet a T-Junction of paths. Turn right. On meeting a gravel track turn left and follow it up to the summit.

The natural cone-shape of the hill was altered by the Normans to make it even steeper. This part of the castle was called a 'motte' and a wooden tower would have been built on its flattened top. There is a slight possibility that the tower was built of stone.

Go forward to the tower.

The folly tower dates from about 1760 and stands on the site of an earlier 12th century chapel. At the foot of the north side a few of the original chapel stones are still visible, standing out squarely from the round base.

The chapel was dedicated to St Michael the Archangel, a dedication often given to hilltop churches (eg. on Glastonbury Tor). It may suggest that the hill had earlier pagan associations and that the warrior Archangel was chosen to represent the victory of good over evil.

Climb the tower. There are excellent views: south are the Dorset Downs, north is a fine view of The Borough and Montacute House itself. Retrace your steps to the foot of the tower once more.

The wooded area, to the south-west of the motte, at the foot of the steep slope, was the castle 'bailey', which would have contained the main living and working quarters. They were placed there because the top of the motte was too small to accomodate the whole population of the castle. The whole complex of motte and bailey would have been surrounded by a wooden palisade.

Return to the gravel track and descend the hill until you reach a gate into a field. Cross it and turn immediately left and keep the hedge and hill on your left. Note the ancient, sunken track in the field below you on the right. You soon meet the path you used to walk up from the abbey gatehouse. Return to The Borough.

The ruins of Glastonbury Abbey.

Legendary Glastonbury

St John's church – Abbey ruins – St Benignus' church Wearyall Hill
Pomparles Bridge – Chalice Well – Glastonbury Tor
Bove Town – High Street.

This walk of 4 miles takes place in and around perhaps the greatest centre of myths and legends in the whole of the British Isles, some would say in western Europe. Concentrated on Glastonbury are traditions and claims, some of which are fictional, others deeply moving. It is a strange but fascinating place.

Time: 2 ½ hours.

Starting point: The car-park in The Archers Way (alternatively Butt Close) behind the High Street. (Grid ref: 501 391).

Facilities: Glastonbury has a full range of facilities ranging from excellent pubs and restaurants to tea rooms and supermarkets. There are also many bookshops whose shelves reflect the often esoteric character of the town.

Problems: Climbs up Wearyall Hill and Glastonbury Tor. But these are the 'heights' of legend and well worth the effort.

Background: The story of Glastonbury is a complex tangle of history, archaeology, legend and pure hype! Its Arthurian legends – dominating much of this walk – are among the most famous in the world. All of which are made more complicated by being tangled up with ancient and modern claims and theories that have little connection with reality.

Glastonbury lies on the edge of the Somerset Levels and in the third and second centuries BC the Celtic inhabitants built waterside settlements to the west of the present town. There is only a little evidence for Roman settlement, though there may have been a Celtic Christian community before the arrival of the Saxons. There definitely was a Dark Age settlement on the Tor and by the 7th century the incoming Anglo-Saxons had established an abbey on its present site, which may have replaced an earlier one.

In the later 10th century the great Saxon reformer Dunstan reorganised the abbey and it went on to become one of the most wealthy in the country, claiming to be the burial place of numerous saints

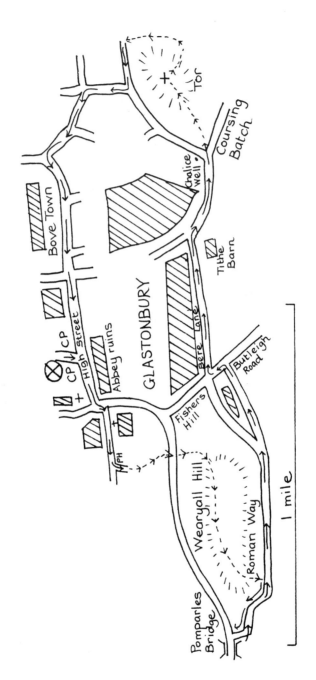

Tor

Coursing Batch

Chalice Well

Bove Town

Tithe Barn

CP

CP

High Street

Abbey ruins

GLASTONBURY

Bere Lane

Butleigh Road

PH

Fishers Hill

Wearyall Hill

Roman Way

Pomparles Bridge

1 mile

The Tribunal, Glastonbury.

and of Arthur himself. The abbey was dissolved in 1539 and its abbot hung on the Tor.

Directions
After parking in the car-parks in either The Archers Way or Butt Close, walk back to the High Street. Walk down it until you come to St John's Church on your right.

St John's church has in its churchyard two thorn trees (cuttings from an older tree) which since 1677 have been claimed to have been planted by Joseph of Arimathea, reputed to be the founder of the first Christian church in Britain. Joseph's fame lay in the fact that he had asked for the body of Christ after the crucifixion and had given up his own tomb for the burial. The thorn is a variety of common hawthorn, which can flower at Christmas as well as in May.

The church tower (at 41 metres) is the second tallest in Somerset and the oldest part of the church – the north chapel of St Katherine – dates from the 12th century. This chapel contains a stained-glass window depicting the life of Joseph of Arimathea, who is shown holding two cruets containing the blood and sweat of Jesus. In Glastonbury Abbey tradition the cruets replaced the Holy Grail, which in other medieval legends was thought to have been the vessel in which Christ's blood was collected by Joseph. The windows date from 1936.

Carrying on down the High Street.

On the right you pass a fine old building signposted as Glastonbury Tribunal. Tradition claims this as the courthouse of the nearby abbey but in reality it is a medieval merchant's house dating from about 1400. It is now a museum, whose collection includes finds from the Iron Age Glastonbury 'lake villages' and is well worth a visit.

Near the bottom of the High Street is the George and Pilgrim Hotel, originally built to accomodate medieval visitors to the abbey. What are actually stone cellars beneath the pub are locally claimed to be the remains of a tunnel used by the abbot for secret (and presumably sinful) visits to the town.

At the bottom of the High Street cross the road and follow the street as it bends to the left and becomes Magdalene Street. The main entrance to the abbey ruins is off this street. There is a small charge for entry and there is an excellent visitors' centre.

The ruins nearest the visitors' centre are those of the Lady Chapel, also known from the early 16th century as St Joseph's Chapel. In the late 10th century the writer of the Life of Dunstan claimed that the first Christians to arrive at Glastonbury found a church already mysteriously built there. William of Malmesbury, writing in about 1130, recorded a claim that the disciples of Christ had built it. In his day an ancient wattle building stood on the site of the now ruined Lady Chapel. It was called the 'Old Church' and had been surrounded with plank walls and a lead roof to protect it. Later fire and rebuilding have removed all archaeological evidence of this church.

Go down the steps – signposted 'St Joseph's chapel and well'.

By 1200, popular legends claimed that Joseph of Arimathea had travelled to western Europe and that his followers had gone on to 'the Vales of Avaron [Avalon]' with the Holy Grail. Other legends claimed that Joseph himself had carried the Grail to Britain. This vessel had earlier appeared in French romances as a magical dish revealed to Arthur's knights, but quickly developed into the cup used by Jesus at the last supper.

Glastonbury Abbey was traditionally founded by St Philip, but in the mid 13th century the monks started replacing this with the story that Joseph was the builder of the first church on the site. By the 14th century this had become the 'official' version, though the grail had been replaced by two cruets.

Coming back up from the crypt, notice the hollow in the bank to your right. The plaque there shows that this was the eastern limit of the 'Old Church'. Go back to the Lady Chapel but this time take the wooden walkway through the chapel, looking down into the crypt as you walk through. On the other side stop and look diagonally left. About halfway between the Lady Chapel and the drop in ground level a remarkable discovery was once made – or so the abbey claimed.

In 1184 the abbey suffered a fire which destroyed the Old Church. It was a severe blow, but a short time later, in 1191, the monks claimed to have unearthed the body of King Arthur and his queen in the spot ahead of you. By this time Arthur was already a popular hero and the claim that the abbey had found his bones attracted many pilgrims, substantially adding to its wealth.

The monks claimed that a lead cross was found with the two bodies and that it read: 'Here lies the famous King Arthur with Guinevere his second wife, in the island of Avallonia' (There are disagreements over the exact wording, some accounts miss out Guinevere.) The name Avalon was unknown before the early 12th century, when the writer Geoffrey of Monmouth made it the mysterious place where King Arthur was taken to have his wounds tended after his last battle – though he did not locate it in any real place. Later, Gerald of Wales (writing in 1192) linked it to Glastonbury, recording the monks' claim to have found Arthur's body here the previous year. This identification of Avalon with Glastonbury was soon followed by other medieval writers and the claim has persisted to the present day.

Walk along the wall of the Lady Chapel towards the main ruins. Turn left into the paved area and then right up the steps. Walk ahead across the grass towards the huge ruined archway.

Immediately beyond the broken arch is a paved area and the outline of a grave.

Arthur and Guinevere's 'remains' were first moved to a chapel in the south aisle and later to a black marble tomb, where they became a great attraction. In 1278 King Edward I and his queen inspected the bones, and they were placed in a tomb in front of the high altar.

Walk back through the ruins to the main gate again. Coming out from the abbey, cross Magdalene Street, turn right and then take the first left down Benedict Street. After about 100 metres is the church of St Benedict on the left. It was earlier the church of St Benignus.

The earliest surviving part of the church of St Benignus/Benedict dates from the 14th century, the rest is from the early 16th century. However, tradition claims that the earliest church on this site was built in 1091, when the bones of the saint were brought here from Meare.

Walk on, passing the King Arthur pub on the left. Turn left into Fairfield Gardens and walk to the end of the road and along the footpath to Safeways supermarket. At Safeways turn right and walk up to the main road to Street. Cross it and turn right. After the last house on the left go through the metal kissing gate into the field. Walk up the hill making for the thorn tree and seat on the ridge.

Before you ascend the hill you cross the route of what seems to be an abandoned canal, which may be late Saxon in date. Other suggestions are that it may have been a 13th century watercourse linked to mills, or an exceptionally long medieval fishpond. Its course was between the road and the newly planted row of trees in the field.

Walk up to the solitary thorn tree.

Wearyall Hill is traditionally the place where Joseph of Arimathea stopped and first looked down onto the site of Glastonbury. In legend his staff took root as he rested on the hill, exclaiming 'We are weary, all'. This particular tradition can be dated no earlier than the early 18th century. There is still a thorn tree growing on the hill but the name is really a corruption of Wirral Hill, meaning 'isolated land where bog-myrtle grows'.

There are excellent views of the town, Tor and moors crossed by rhynes (drainage ditches). Walk on along the ridge towards Street, keeping the copse to the right. Follow the slope down to a gate (another copse on left). Cross stile and walk to the end of the field, with a new bungalow ahead. Turn left and follow the path down to the road. At the road (Roman Way) turn right and follow the road downhill to where it joins the main road before a bridge.

This is Pomparles Bridge, a corruption of the Latin 'pons periculosus' (the dangerous bridge), which in Arthurian legend is the bridge which Lancelot crosses to rescue his lover – Arthur's wife, Guinevere. The original name for the bridge in this vicinity was simply Street Bridge and the present name is probably a late medieval invention – when the Arthurian legends were flourishing – given to a new bridge, built here in the 13th century. The 16th century writer John Leland was told that this was the spot where Excalibur was thrown back into the water after Arthur's fatal last battle.

Walk back up Roman Way. Follow it to its end at a mini round-about. Walk on ahead along Tor View Avenue until it meets But-leigh Road. Turn left and then right into Bere Lane (named after a 16th century abbot). Follow the road (pavement on the left hand side) to its end, where it meets Chilkwell Street.

The medieval priory barn on the right, at the junction with Chilkwell Street, once belonged to the abbey. It probably dates from the 14th century and was originally thatched. It testifies to the wealth of agricultural products produced by the surrounding estate of the abbey. It now houses the Somerset Rural Life Museum and includes fine collections reconstructing life in the Somerset countryside. It greatly repays a visit and is most enjoyable.

After the abbey barn turn right into Chilkwell Street. Follow the raised pavement on the left side of the road. Continue to the last house on the left: Chalice Well.

A major spring feeds the water courses of a very pleasant garden here. There is a small charge for entry. The spring is reached by way of a shaft with a wrought iron decorated cover. The shaft actually goes through a 12th century wellhouse, now buried by silt. The spring is known as Chalice Well and is another of Glastonbury's high points of legend. According to local tradition its water runs red because of the Holy Grail which lies somewhere underground. In fact minerals colour the water.

The legend can be dated back no earlier than the 19th century. The present name is actually derived from Chilkwell, as in nearby Chilkwell Street: it was recorded as Chalcewelle, in 1210.

After Chalice Well, turn left up Wellhouse Lane. Almost

immediately there is a path on the right leading from the road up to the Tor. It is before Berachah House. Follow the path through the copse. Go through the stone stile. Ahead is the Tor.

The Tor is astonishing. It rises to 158 metres (518 feet above sea level) and its sides are terraced. Its top is made of a hard limestone. This has protected its lower layers and stopped their erosion.

Follow the path up to the next gate. Notice how the hillside ahead is terraced.

These are either medieval strip lynchets used in farming, or the remains of a three dimensional prehistoric sacred maze, depending on your viewpoint. There is no conclusive evidence either way.

Go through the iron stile. Keep any dogs on a lead as sheep graze here. Follow the well marked path upwards, along the flank of the Tor.

The earliest linking of Arthur with Glastonbury was by Caradoc of Llancarfan (about 1140) in his book, *The Life of St Gildas*. In this, Arthur's wife, Guinevere, was carried off by Melwas, king of the Summer Region (Somerset). Arthur besieged him at Glastonbury and the abbot obtained her release.

Follow the concrete steps upwards to the seat. From here there is a fine view back to Wearyall Hill and ahead to the summit. Walk on up.

There was a Dark Age settlement (6th century AD) on the top, either the outpost of a local chieftain, or a pre-Saxon Christian religious community – the evidence is ambiguous. In later centuries the Tor seems to have served as a retreat for monks from the abbey down below.

On the summit you reach a church tower.

The ruined church of St Michael on the Tor was destroyed by an earthquake in 1275. The surviving tower dates from the 14th century with 15th century additions. In 1539 the last abbot, Richard Whiting, and two monks were hanged on the summit. Whiting was charged with theft but his real 'crime' was clearly resisting Henry VIII's dissolution of the monasteries. Despite being in his seventies he was shown no mercy and was hauled to the summit on a sledge, meeting his death there bravely.

From the Tor take the steps down on the south-eastern side. The

Glastonbury Tor.

path winds round the eastern flank and eventually the track leads to the lane on the northern side of the Tor. This is Stone Down Lane. Turn left and follow the lane to where it veers to the right. The road goes on ahead and becomes Wellhouse Lane. However, you turn right and follow the lane to a crossroads, one arm of which is a track on the right. Continue to follow the road, which bends to the left into Wick Hollow. Follow the lane until a road joins it from the right. This is called Old Wells Road. Ahead is Bove Town, which was on the original route into Glastonbury from Wells as it was only after 1782 that the present Wells road was built. Follow Bove Town downhill to Glastonbury. At the bottom of the hill you will find the top of High Street ahead of you. Follow it to where The Archers Way leads off on the right to the car parks.

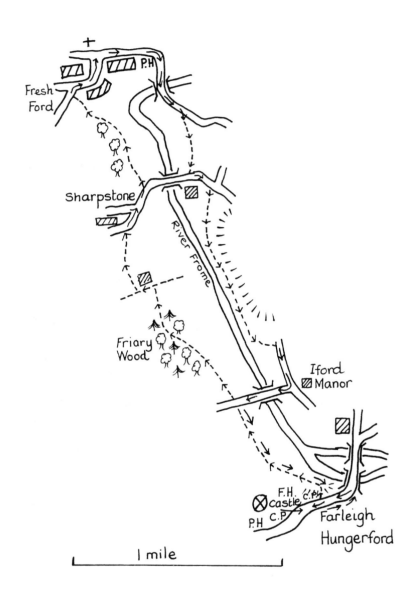

Fresh Ford

P.H

Sharpstone

River Frome

Friary Wood

Iford Manor

F.H. C.P.
castle
P.H C.P
Farleigh Hungerford

|⟍――――――――――――――――――⟍| 1 mile

Wool, Wealth and Murder

Farleigh Hungerford castle – Sharpstone – Freshford
Iford – Farleigh Hungerford

A 5 mile walk, which explores the beautiful valley of the river Frome and includes an excellent example of a ruined castle, the picturesque stone-built village of Freshford and fascinating remains of the north-east Somerset woollen industry.

Time: 2 ½ hours.

Starting Point: The car-park of Farleigh Hungerford castle. (Grid ref: 801 575).

Facilities: The pub (The Castle) at Farleigh and a small range of facilities at Freshford, including a pub (The Inn), offering a very varied and well priced menu, and village shop.

Problems: No problems, except a short, steep climb down from Farleigh Castle.

Background: The course of the River Frome is one of the better kept secrets of historic Somerset. The narrow valley is secluded and wooded and it is hard to imagine that in the 13th century this was probably the most important industrial river valley in the West of England. A large number of fulling mills – the last stage in the production of woollen cloth – were sited along the Frome. It was wealth from the wool trade which helped pay for the castle at Farleigh Hungerford.

By 1500 the main cloth produced in the area was called 'white broadcloth'. During the 17th century it was replaced by a type of cloth called 'Spanish cloth', or 'Spanish medley'. Made from fine wool, this was a lighter weight cloth made in a wide range of colours. From the 18th century the industry was hit by competition from Yorkshire and abroad. By the end of the 19th century it had almost vanished.

Directions
Park in the car-park of Farleigh Hungerford Castle. A small charge is payable to English Heritage to visit the site. Alternatively, park in the small space outside the castle and overlooking the valley.

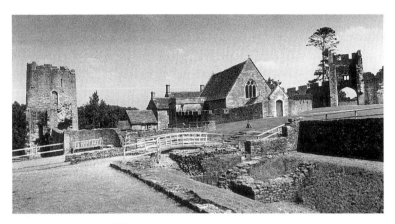

Farleigh Hungerford Castle.

Farleigh Hungerford Castle lies on a site overlooking the valley and in a position to make the most of its trade. Breeding flocks of Hungerford sheep were pastured at Wellow, others grazed the western downs of Salisbury Plain above the Hungerford's Wiltshire manor and woolstore at Heytesbury, on the Wylye. All of this woollen empire was coordinated from the head estate at Farleigh where the wool was sold to local clothiers.

Walking from the castle car-park you enter the Outer Bailey.

The castle originally consisted of the inner court to the left. It was built by Sir Thomas Hungerford, who was the first Speaker of the House of Commons, in about 1370. The outer court, in which you are standing, was added by his son Walter, after 1420. The ditch between the two was a dry moat.

Walk on, to the sign saying Ticket Office.

The church in front of you was originally the parish church of St Leonard. Sir Walter included it in his outer court and made it the castle chapel. He built another one for the parish, to the south. Inside are excellent 14th, or 15th century wall paintings of St George and a kneeling knight. In the north chapel are tombs of Sir Edward Hungerford (died 1648) and his wife Margaret and, inside rails, Sir Thomas Hungerford (died 1398) and his wife Joan.

In the vault under the church are the lead coffins of six adults and two children. A flight of steps, outside the church, leads down to the vault. East of the chapel, beyond a small courtyard, is a medieval priest's house, dating from 1430. It was extended in the late 17th century and now houses a museum.

After exploring the church, cross the bridge into the Inner Bailey.

Inside the inner court the ground plans of many rooms are visible. All were destroyed during the 18th century. A well and nearby sink still survive as does the main drain.

From the Inner Bailey go over to the tower overlooking the car park.

In 1522 the lord of the castle – Edward Hungerford I – died leaving his wealth to his widow, Agnes, his second wife. By September she was under arrest, charged with arranging the murder of her first husband, John Cotell, and the burning of his body in the castle furnace. In 1523 she was hanged at Tyburn. So, did Edward die of natural causes, or was he too murdered?

This south-western tower (the Lady Tower) is where Edward's son, another Walter, imprisoned his third wife for four years, in the 16th century. She claimed that she was given little to eat and that attempts were made to poison her. In 1540 Walter was executed for 'treason and unnatural vice'.

Leave the castle by its main entrance/exit, and look back at the gateway.

The main gateway is linked to a causeway built to replace a drawbridge in about 1610. Look back to where, above the gateway, is the newly restored sickle badge of the Hungerford family. The two holes on either side were for the drawbridge chains.

The castle is not a ruined product of the Civil War. It was held for the king by one Hungerford (John) but surrendered to his half brother, Sir Edward, who fought for parliament, in 1645. The ruined state is due to the debts of another Sir Edward Hungerford, 'the Spendthrift', who in 1686 sold the castle: by 1701 it had been stripped and was in ruins

Standing outside the castle look ahead, along the valley of the Frome.

The mill at Farleigh is first mentioned in 1548; it seems to have been a fulling mill and a corn mill. A fulling mill was where cloth was beaten in water, mixed with fuller's earth and urine, or 'sig'(later oil soap) to shrink and thicken the cloth. After this it was stretched and dried. Then teazles were pulled over the cloth to 'raise the nap', and the cloth was sheared smooth.

Go to the edge of the slope and look down.

Below is the site of the mill. It included an edge-tool mill, as a Trowbidge shear grinder rented it in the 1750s. The shears themselves were probably made at the iron works at Nunney and were locally used for finishing the surface of the cloth. Burnt down in 1798, it was rebuilt as a four-storeyed shearing and dyeing factory. Nearby was a separate fulling mill.

Cross the road (taking great care) and follow the pavement downhill to the first bridge.

The original mills were water driven and below you is the mill stream, or leat, which powered the mill. It was led off the River Frome at a weir about 250 metres upstream from the bridge and although the flow of water is not fast, the machinery was powerful. In the 1790s a young Freshford girl fell under the fulling hammers to her death. Many country mills remained powered by water well into the 19th century, but at Farleigh, James Fussell of Mells had a steam engine installed by 1823 which supplemented the two water wheels.

Return up the hill to the castle, taking great care when crossing the road.

The 1871 census shows that the success of the mill led to an increase in population at a time when the West Country cloth industry was in decline. In the 1850s it was claimed that the finest doeskins in the world were produced by Charles Salter and Co. at Farleigh Hungerford. Farleigh Mill survived until 1910, and most of the buildings have now vanished from the site.

At the rough car-park outside the gate, take the steep flight of uneven steps down the slope. Take care.

Here under the castle walls, downstream from the main factory was a separate fulling mill. This was probably the site of the original mill.

Follow the path to a gravel track. Turn left onto the track. The mill stream is on the right. Turn right, off the track and follow Footpath signs.

To your right the land rises steeply from the river. On the top of the hill is the site of the lost villages of Wittenham and Rowley. Wittenham was first recorded in a charter of 1001. Later it was sometimes called Rowley and, since mentions of Rowley gradually replaced Wittenham, they were probably two adjacent settlements, one of which had declined. The other one was not to survive either, as in 1428 the parish was amalgamated with Farleigh Hungerford and now nothing remains of the villages with their church and mill.

Cross the stream, using the footbridge, and over a stile into the field. Turn right and follow the path. Cross another stile. A mill leat joins the River Frome on the right. Follow the path, with the river on your right.

Notice the pill-box over the Frome. The valley has a large number of these machine-gun posts from World War II, most of which are overlooked and would have been very hard to defend.

Head for the gate ahead with stile. (Good views back to the castle). Head for the gate across the next field, with an iron kissing gate beside it. Dog Kennel Farm is ahead and to the left. Cross the wooden stile ahead. Pass to the right of the farm; notice the weir on the river. At this point the mill-stream of Iford Mill leaves the river. The iron sluice gates were built to control its flow. Walk to the gate ahead and cross the metalled road, following a way-marked foot-path into the opposite field. Iford Mill is on your right (touched on later in the walk).

This area of wooded valley was terrorised in the late 18th century by a notorious highwayman, who was finally caught and hanged at Freshford.

Follow the hedgeline, on your left, to where it meets the wood.

Friary Wood, was the site of the quarters of the lay brothers of Hinton Charterhouse priory. These were the members of the community who worked on the estate of the priory. The name of the wood preserves the link with the past (from the Middle English and Old French word 'frere', or 'brother').

Walk on, keeping the wood on your left, until you come to a gate and stile leading into the wood. Go over the stile and follow the track through the wood. Go over the next stile, out of the wood and into a field. Cross another stile and walk on to meet a track by a scattered settlement. Turn left, uphill onto the track, and then, after 30 metres, turn right off the track, up the hill to another stile. Follow the bridleway, with the wood on your left and the valley below on your right. When you reach a large building ahead of you, stop.

In the late eighteenth century, the partners Moggridge and Joyce moved from their rented mill at Avoncliff to a new factory (Dunkirk

Factory) on one of the streams flowing into the Frome, at Freshford. It is this former mill which is ahead of you. In 1833 the government's First Report of the Factory Commissioners condemned the excessive hours worked by young employees here. Of all the mills examined by the commissioner, in Gloucestershire, Wiltshire and Somerset, it was the only one working a 15 hour day (5am – 8pm), though no children under 12 were employed.

Turn left and follow the path uphill and through the gate into the wood, for about 100 metres. At the top of the rise stop.

On the right are the ponds used to build up a head of water from the spring which rises at the end of the little combe. (The ponds are now a fish farm.) This provided the power which ran the mill. Such a small stream though would have been unable to power the factory in dry weather. Changes were needed.

Return to the former Dunkirk Mill, retracing your steps.

Steam power reached the Dunkirk Factory by 1810 and gig mills and shearing frames (mechanised ways of finishing cloth) were in use in Freshford by 1813. Despite this, the mills faced increased competition from the north of England from the 1830s and the owners of the Dunkirk Mill went bankrupt in 1824.

Walk on, with the ex-mill on the left, following the track to a metalled road. Up the hill is Sharpstone. At the road turn right and follow the road downhill. Freshford Mill lies across the river on the right.

Prosperity in the 18th century led to an expansion of the existing 16th century fulling mill, which had once belonged to Hinton Charterhouse priory. In 1795 the mill was bought from the Methuen family by Samuel Perkins for £2000. Two large wings were added by 1796. The original mill also included a grist mill, used for the grinding of corn and malt for brewing. This combination of mills was quite common.

In the later 1830s the mill was restarted after having lain idle for some years. However, in the 1870s Moore and Edmunds, its owners, went bankrupt. In 1879 Freshford Mill was sold to makers of flock, used in mattresses. As such it survived until after World War II. Its great days were over. In 1945 it became a rubber factory and the discolouration of many of the walls is due to the carbon-black used in the process of making rubber. This industry has now relocated to Trowbridge.

The River Frome at Freshford.

At the bridge, leave the road and follow the path ahead. Pass another pill-box on the right. Cross two stiles and follow the path along the steep, wooded riverbank. At the top of the slope ignore the iron stile on the right. Instead, walk on to the road, a high wall on your right.

Ahead lies Freshford, a village whose entire character was decided by the wool industry. Much of the weaving was done in the village, while the more complicated fulling and finishing of cloth was carried out in the nearby mills. Relations between the weavers and the mill owners were often poor. By the end of the 18th century new textile machines were appearing in the area and meeting great opposition from weavers using older methods. An attempt to introduce the Flying Shuttle to Freshford had to be abandoned in 1800; a similar attempt in Trowbridge had led to a riot in 1792.

In 1803 *The Gloucester Journal* carried a report of workers at Freshford collecting arms and ammunition to resist new machinery. They were planning, it was claimed, to fight the army who were protecting the mill owners!

At the road turn right and cross another road on a bend, to the pavement, following the road signposted 'Bradford on Avon'.

Walk on to the church. On the way, notice the interesting lion statue over the gate on your right.

Diagonally opposite the church is Ivythorpe House, with a fine early Georgian front with Tuscan Pillars. Down the hill, to the left, the Victorian brewery is now given over to housing and offices.

You however turn right and follow the main road downhill. Notice the 18th century fire insurance badge on the wall of the house on the right, just before the Station sign.

Facing up the street, another house possesses early 18th century iron railings and the centre window on the first floor has an unusual heavy arching keystone.

At this point cross the road, as the pavement changes sides, and walk on.

The Inn, called the New Inn as early as 1885, dates from 1713. Notice the fine mullioned windows under hood moulds. It is a fine point to break the walk and the food is excellent.

Cross the bridge.

Freshford Bridge is a late medieval one. In 1540 the Tudor historian Leland described its 'faire new arches of stone'.

Follow the road. As the road bends left, go over a stile on the right. Walk ahead towards Freshford Mill, past a disused stile. Cross another stile into the road. Turn left and follow the road for 40 metres to where another minor road joins it from the left. At this point, turn right into a field, over a stile. Walk straight ahead. At the end of the field, by the hedge corner, the path leads off on the left. The river is on your right and a thick hedge and a small cliff on your left.
   The cliff on the left becomes less steep. Cross a stile and go diagonally left up the slope to where a low stone stile is set into the hedge. Go over, onto the road, turning right and down to Iford (By the next gate on the right notice another machine-gun post down by the river).

Iford means 'ford by an island', from the Old English words 'ieg' (island) and 'ford'. Iford Manor on the left, facing the river, is beautifully situated, tucked away into the wooded hillside. Its front dates from 1725-30. On the left, the two cottages – with a fine oriel

Iford Manor, with the statue of Britannia facing upstream.

window – were once stables. The manor here was bought by the Hungerfords in 1369 and held for three centuries.

Its famous gardens were laid out by its owner Harold Peto, assisted by Edwin Lutyens, after 1899. By 1914 the character of the gardens had been created, mixing trees and shrubs with classical (and later) architecture and sculptures. Many of these features are terraced into the hillside, giving the gardens a Mediterranean feel. From the late 1960s the head-gardener, Leon Butler, both restored the original gardens and developed them; adding, for example, a Japanese garden. The gardens are now open to the public at specified times.

Cross the bridge.

The bridge is a medieval one, with two arches. There is a tradition that it was built in 1400 by the monks from Hinton Charterhouse. The unusual figure of Britannia on the breakwater was placed here by Peto. Local tradition says it once looked the other way but was turned to face upstream because Britannia should face the waves!

Walk on.

On the right is the long, originally one storey, Iford Mill. The archway that channels the mill leat under the building can clearly be seen.

Beyond the mill you complete the circuit of this walk. Turn left and follow the riverside walk back to Farleigh Hungerford.

At the weir look ahead and right to the farm on the ridge. This is now Lodge Farm. This was the site of the falconry belonging to the Hungerfords. The small stone falconry mews still survives and looks down on the valley where the Hungerford lords once hunted and where you have walked.

The deserted medieval village of Nether Adber, showing the remains of its ridge-and-furrow fields.

Lost and Shrunken Villages of South Somerset

Mudford – Hinton – Nether Adber – Mudford
(Extension to West Mudford and Mudford Terry)

This walk of 4 miles (with a possible 1½ mile extension) takes place in a southern Somerset parish famous for its deserted and shrunken settlements. It explores the remains of once thriving communities that exist no longer.

Time: 2 hours.

Starting point: Mudford parish church, near Yeovil. (Grid ref: 574 199).

Facilities: Limited village facilities in Mudford itself. A wide range of facilities in Yeovil, 2 miles distance.

Problems: No problems except for a quarter mile walk on the A359, which requires care.

Background: Mudford parish contains some of the best evidence of deserted and shrunken settlements in the whole of Somerset. There were five different manors here at the time of Domesday Book and the largest was given, with the church, to Montacute Priory in 1102 by its founder William, Count of Mortain. During the next four hundred years a number of these settlements declined, though their remains can still be traced in the modern landscape.

In the Middle Ages the ploughland in the parish was organised in large open-fields, which would have been divided into strips, with farmers owning land scattered across the various fields. These strips have left a corduroy-like pattern of dips and ridges ('ridge and furrow') still recognisable today.

From the 16th century onwards efforts were made to break up these large arable fields and instead graze sheep in smaller, hedged fields. This increased the profit enjoyed by landlords but drove many villagers from the land. Another problem was a lack of available land to cope with a growing population, and at Mudford there were complaints that the soil fertility had declined. The reasons for the failure of these settlements is thus complicated, and

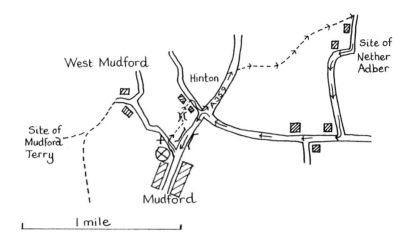

is often blamed on plague with very little evidence to justify the claim.

Directions

Park in the lane beside Mudford church.

On the left of the path leading to the church there is the interesting tomb of William Whitby (died 1635) and his wife Anne (died 1617). The lead plaque records how he left £5 a year 'forever to ye poore' and has two fascinating engravings of figures in 17th century costume. The church itself contains fine examples of 17th century pews.

Opposite the church a small iron gate leads into the field. Go up the stone steps and walk ahead, keeping the river on your right.

On your left, a quarter of a mile away, are the remains of West Mudford. Deserted 'tofts', where houses once stood are closest to the road. Their plots of lands would have run down to the River Yeo.

West Mudford is now a scatter of farms but was once much larger. It was first mentioned in a legal case of 1271, when a woman named Denyse de Romeseye was accused of denying Robert de la Mare his right to pasture livestock in West Mudford. It was obviously a tiny settlement even then and by 1838 consisted only of a scatter of houses and gardens (crofts).

Follow the riverbank to where a wooden bridge, over broken stone piers, crosses a side channel.

The footbridge crosses an abandoned mill leat formed from a cut made across a loop in the River Yeo. Note the drop of water on the left, to increase the power of the mill – now vanished.

Beyond the footbridge, cross the stile and walk to the iron gate ahead and to the left. Cross the River Yeo by the small bridge. On reaching the road stop.

The modern settlement of Hinton is made up of the scatter of farm buildings here and further west along the road. This modern road was once the village street. Hinton is first mentioned in the Lay Subsidy of 1327, though an earlier mention of a place called Estinton (in 1316) may refer to it by another name. There was once a chapel and a moated manor house, which fell into ruins in the 15th century.

The remains of the manor house are in the field opposite. Cross the road to look through the gate into the field.

In 1838 the name of this field was recorded as 'Courthay and Site of Cardinal Holsey's palace'. This derives from a local legend claiming that the site belonged to Wolsey, Henry VIII's chancellor. In fact, Wolsey had been Rector of Limington, a little to the west.

Mudford Church.

To reach the next site involves a short distance on the road. Follow the road right towards its junction with the A359 Yeovil – Marston Magna road. Note the fine thatch of Green Close Cottage on your right and the mill gear set into the window. As you walk there is slight ridge and furrow in the field to your right. At the A359 turn left and follow it for a quarter of a mile. Take care – there is no footpath. Pass a lay-by on the left. About 150 metres beyond is a new iron gate on the right. Cross it into the field. Walk diagonally left towards a gate in the middle distance, crossing a stream on the way. Go through the gate and walk ahead keeping the house ahead to your right. Note ridge and furrow on your right. Pass the house on your right and go through the gate to left of pond. Walk towards the bungalow ahead, keeping it on your right. The earthworks on the right are the remains of Nether Adber. Aim for the wooden gate to the left of the power lines. Go over it into the lane;turn right and walk down it.

You are entering the northern part of the deserted village of Nether Adber. The lane ahead runs right through the site of the village and was the village street. Adber was mentioned in Domesday Book (1086) when it was called Ettebere. It had been owned since before the Norman Conquest by a Saxon named Siward 'the fowler'. Confusingly there were two other settlements also called Adber. By 1303 it seems to have been called Little Adber. Later in the 14th century there is mention of it as Nether Adber. The name means 'lower' Adber.

Look into the field on the right, where power lines cross the road. This is the field you walked across earlier.

On the 1838 Tithe Map this was called 'Chapel Hay with ancient ruins', and is almost certainly the site of the village church, first mentioned in 1351. The large bank enclosing this field is still noticeable and, as late as the 1960s, contained evidence of a moated manor house and fishponds.

Walk down the lane, past the bungalow on the right.

On your right there are the remains of house platforms, and the boundaries of crofts. There are also hollow-ways which must have linked the houses to the main street and the fields. These remains show as raised and dipped areas in the pasture.

The lane bends sharply right – stop.

The edge of the field in front is marked by a large earth bank on the left – the eastern boundary of the village – and contains the remains of many house platforms.

Follow the lane bending right.

Remains of house foundations and boundary banks can be seen to left and right. At one time the village on either side would have been a thriving community, yet we do not know why it was deserted. Clearly it was not due to the plague, which is often blamed, as it struggled through until the 16th century. Thomas Gerard, writing about the village in 1633, mentioned that 'all of a sudden it sunk'; probably in the 1550s. By 1562 only one person was recorded as living here. The common fields had disappeared; divided up into small fields that survive today.

Stop at Thorny House. It is on your right, at the point where the lane bends sharply left.

Almost immediately opposite Thorny House a hollow-way runs into the field from the lane. This was once an important village street. The fields beyond Thorny House once made up the large North Field and a lot of ridge and furrow survives here.

Follow the lane as it bends sharp left and walk on.

The lane now runs down the boundary ditch at the western side of the village. The last remains of the village itself are in the field on the left, where the houses were probably built of piled turf, or had earth walls. On the right and ahead is what was once the South Field of the village.

Follow the track to where it meets a road. Turn right and follow the road back to the A359. On the way, opposite two bungalows on the left, is a milepost reminding you that since you joined this road, you have been in Dorset. You now return to Somerset. At the A359 turn left and follow the road the short distance back to Mudford church.

The extension
There is a possible extension of this walk. From Mudford church follow the minor road for half a mile to the west. At the first houses of the hamlet of West Mudford turn left off the road onto a side-road. This becomes a track just after you pass The Old Farmhouse, on your right.

This farmhouse has fine stone mullioned windows and a brick and timber corn store, standing on staddle-stones, to keep damp and rats out.

Follow the track, slowly going uphill, until it bends to the left and a side track goes off on the right, by a pile of stone and rubble. Follow this side-track for about 50 metres.

The track leads to the site of the deserted settlement of Mudford Terry, named after Terricus, its 12th century owner. It was later also known as Wood Court. It is not mentioned in the Domesday Book (1086) but this does not mean it did not exist then. The first mention occurs in the *Nomina Villarum* of 1316 which listed villages, along with the name of the lords of the manor, who in this case were Walter and Galfridus de Romeseye. In 1327 the taxation list, called the Lay Subsidy, listed 8 taxpayers here.

At the end of the lane stop at the gate and look into the field.

Since at least 1838 the two fields immediately ahead have been called Wood Court, preserving an alternative 16th century name for the settlement. In 1838 there was a small cottage remaining in the field; now even that has gone, although its well can still be seen immediately to your right, just inside the field and is now capped with a stone slab.

The lane, which now ends at this gate, was once the main route through the village. From this point it ran to the right of the pond and trees, between houses and enclosures north and south of it. About 50 metres in front of where you are standing is a large rectangular enclosure surrounded by an earth bank. It lies beyond and to the left of the trees and was probably the site of a manor house. It may have been a farm, or grange, of Montacute Priory which owned land in Mudford parish. Immediately to your right the hedgeline follows an earth bank, which was probably the eastern boundary of the settlement and which runs right round the site.

Retrace your steps along the lane back to West Mudford and then back to Mudford church.

The Battle of Sedgemoor, 1685

Chedzoy – Parchey – King's Sedgemoor Drain – Langmoor
Westonzoyland – Fowler's Plot – Chedzoy

This walk of 5½ miles explores the modern site of what is probably the most famous and tragic battle in the West Country's history.

Time: Three hours.

Starting Point: Chedzoy. (Grid ref: 342 376)

Facilities: At Westonzoyland there are pubs and village shops.

Problems: None.

Background: James, Duke of Monmouth, landed at Lyme Regis (Dorset) in June 1685 in an attempt to remove his Catholic uncle, James II from the throne. The illegitimate son of Charles II, Monmouth was largely reliant on the cloth working towns of the West Country for his support.

Monmouth was declared king at Taunton and then marched north towards Bristol. However, the gentry did not rise to support him, nor did the massed horsemen arrive which he had been promised by supporters in Wiltshire. He abandoned his planned attack on Bristol after a skirmish with the king's army at Keynsham. Despite a more successful second encounter at Norton St Philip, his revolt began to lose direction and he retraced his steps back into central Somerset.

Reaching Bridgwater on 3rd July, Monmouth saw one last chance to seize the initiative. A farm worker from Chedzoy brought news that the royal troops, under the Earl of Feversham, camped at Westonzoyland, were not entrenched and could be taken by surprise in a night attack. Monmouth took a gamble – and lost.

The Sedgemoor landscape has changed greatly since 1685. Hedged fields have replaced its open pastures and increased drainage has led to the abandonment of many of the 17th century drainage rhynes. Nevertheless, many of the battlefield features can still be approximately located, 'fossilised' in the routes of modern tracks and paths. Consequently, it is still possible to recreate the general movements of the two armies.

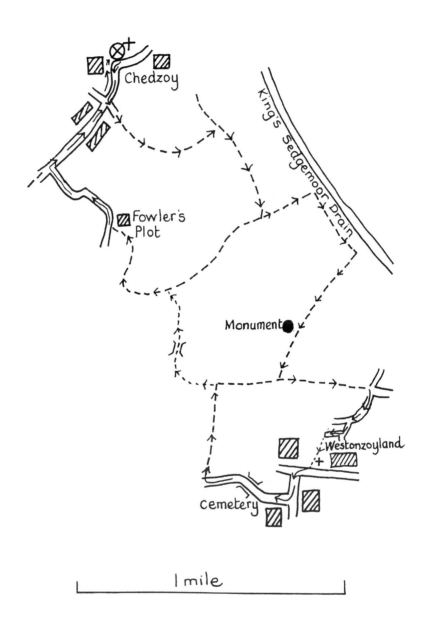

Chedzoy

King's Sedgemoor Drain

Fowler's
Plot

Monument

Westonzoyland

Cemetery

1 mile

James, Duke of Monmouth.

Directions

Park near the church in Chedzoy. Walk down Front Street, opposite the church. You pass a telephone box and a junction with Higher Road on your right. Take the next turning left, up a farm track marked 'Tall Trees'.

The Duke of Monmouth left Bridgwater late on the evening of Sunday, July 5th, with a force of about 4, 000 men. At their head was a local man who promised to lead them across the moor to surprise the king's army at Westonzoyland.

Take the track leading out of Chedzoy onto the moor. At the end of the track go over stile and cross the field to the gate ahead of you. The track beyond is Moor Drove. Stop in the drove.

Monmouth's army moved down this drove, marching from the left. His cavalry, under Lord Grey, had taken the lead and behind them were the Red Regiment, commanded by Lieutenant-Colonel Venner, but led onto the moor by Major Nathaniel Wade, a republican lawyer from Bristol.

Turn right and follow the drove as Monmouth's army did.

Monmouth was keen to skirt Chedzoy, where Feversham had set up a watch. He was spotted however, by two locals, but the watch failed to pass on news of the sighting to the patrolling royal cavalry. For now Monmouth was safe.

The tension must have been intense as the army moved through the darkness: riders not daring to jingle harness, desperately trying

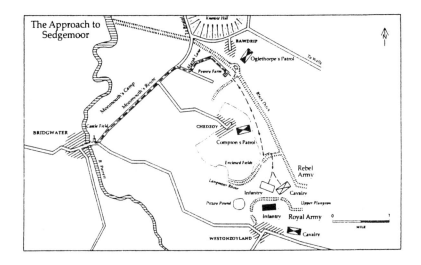

The Approach to Sedgemoor

to keep their mounts calm and quiet, foot soldiers stumbling in the dark. Also there were waggons and carts, hauling at least three guns, under the supervision of the Dutch gunner, Anton Buyse, who before night fell again would be hung outside the church at Weston-zoyland. It would be the first of many such acts of vengeance. But in the dark, victory still seemed possible.

After about 800 metres, the ground rises slightly to the left, about 150 metres away across the field. Between you and this rise is one of the major drainage channels on Sedgemoor.

Monmouth's scout led the army along the southern bank of a drainage rhyne, called in 1685 the Black Ditch. This no longer exists but the King's Sedgemoor Drain – dug in 1794 – follows the approximate course of the old channel.

Walk on down the drove.

Across the Black Ditch (the Sedgemoor Drain) to the left were cavalry patrols of the Life Guards under the command of Colonel Oglethorpe. On the moor to the south of the ditch were patrols of blue-coated troopers of the Royal Regiment of Horse Guards (the Blues) under the command of Major Compton. But neither detected the silent army moving through the dark. Fog deadened noises and cloaked the files of moving men.

The track ends in a T-junction, called Mount Close Batch. The line of the new track, which loops from left to right, marks the line of the drainage ditch called in 1685, Langmoor Rhyne. It fed into the Black Ditch about 150 metres to the left. It was vital that Monmouth cross the Langmoor Rhyne quickly if he was to surprise the king's army while it was still dark. The drainage ditch in front of you was wider and deeper then.

The guide could not find the crossing point, just to the right of here. Perhaps the fog – until now an ally – had become an enemy. In the dark, vital minutes were lost as he frantically searched the bank. The crossing was eventually found but shortly afterwards the army was spotted by a patrolling royal trooper. There was a pistol shot, which some think was discharged by accident by one of Monmouth's men.

We cannot cross here so turn left and follow the new track. Go through a metal gate to the bank of the King's Sedgemoor Drain. Follow the track, bending right, and follow the south bank of the drain.

Monmouth – just to the right of here – pressed on, faster now. It would soon be light and the element of surprise had been lost. His soldiers flooded across the moor to the south. Meanwhile the patrolling trooper alerted the soldiers at Chedzoy and a rider was despatched to Westonzoyland. Racing up and down the course of the rhyne which defended the northern approach to the village, the trooper shouted 'Beat the drums, the enemy is come!'

Cross the bridge and sluice ahead and follow the King's Sedgemoor Drain until, after 100 metres, a track goes off on the right, before you reach a gate and fence. Follow this across Langmoor towards the trees. The track becomes a lane. South of here the enemy was waiting in Westonzoyland, which is now clearly visible (diagonally to the left).

The royal army, under the Earl of Feversham, was camped to the north and west of Westonzoyland. In all it numbered about 2000 foot soldiers and 700 cavalry. Other soldiers, of the Wiltshire Militia, were camped at Middlezoy and Othery to the south-east.

Monmouth's plan had been to send his cavalry into the sleeping camp, followed by his infantry who were to complete the rout. But now the royal army was alerted and any hope of surprise had been lost.

Cross the metal gate and pause.

Royal cavalry, rushed from Chedzoy, crossed the line of this lane, coming from the right, and successfully beat back some of Monmouth's cavalry, just to our left. Meanwhile Grey – about 600 metres to your left – pushed towards Westonzoyland with the rest of the rebel cavalry, trying to penetrate the royal defences and fulfil his part of the disintegrating plan.

Walk on down the lane, named Langmoor, or Battlefield, Drove. Monmouth's infantry were now moving up on your right, heading towards Westonzoyland. It was now about 2 o'clock in the morning. With the Sedgemoor Monument (found on the right side of the lane) behind you, look east towards Bussex Farm, the buildings to the left of the trees.

The village and its royalist defenders were protected on the north and west by a large drainage ditch called the Bussex Rhyne. It has now been drained and filled in but its approximate course is marked by a lane running east-west. This runs to the right of Bussex Farm and between you and the village. The lane you are in joins it about 300 metres ahead. The rhyne swung south to the west of the village and its course is marked by a path linking the track ahead of you, to another lane running north from the modern A372. We can use these tracks to imagine the course of what was then a deep drainage ditch.

Look towards Bussex Farm, about a third of a mile from you. Somewhere near the farm was a crossing point of the rhyne – called the Upper Plungeon. It was crucial that Grey find it and cross, but he could not locate the spot. From that moment, Monmouth's army – having now reached where you are standing – was doomed.

Grey rode back towards you, along the northern edge of the rhyne (the modern east-west lane). He was exposed to the fire of the awakened royal army; he panicked and fled with most of his cavalry off to our left. Those remaining finally found the Upper Plungeon but could not hold it. Left to face the enemy, musket and cannon fire tore across the rhyne, horses and riders falling beneath the onslaught.

Begin to walk on down the drove in the direction of Westonzoyland.

Facing Monmouth's army beyond Bussex Farm (ahead and diagonally to our left) was Dumbarton's Royal Regiment of Foot, led by Lieutenant-Colonel Douglas. Along the line of the rhyne -from left to right as we look – were more field guns, then the First Regiment of Foot Guards, under Colonel Grafton. Ahead and to out right, on the bend of the Bussex Rhyne, were the Coldstream Guards, under Lieutenant-Colonel Sackville.

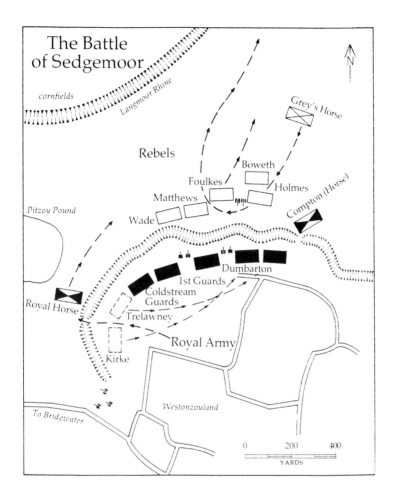

The Battle
of Sedgemoor

cornfields

Langmoor Rhine

N

Grey's Horse

Rebels

Boweth

Foulkes

Holmes

Matthews

Compton (Horse)

Pitzoy Pound

Wade

Dumbarton

1st Guards

Royal Horse

Coldstream
Guards

Trelawney

Royal Army

Kirke

To Bridgwater

Westonzoyland

0   200   400

YARDS

Move on down the lane ahead to where it meets the east-west lane.

Most of Grey's horsemen had now left the field, riding up towards
you and back the way you have come. However, Monmouth did not
abandon the attempt to storm the enemy. Somehow he rallied his
frightened infantry and moved them on against the royal troops
who were now waiting for them, ahead.

At the T-junction stop. You are now on the line of the Bussex
Rhyne. It followed the lane to your left and right.

Dawn was approaching. For the second time, Monmouth's army came up to the rhyne (the north side of this lane), firing muskets and their three cannon into the Scots soldiers of Dunbarton's regiment on the other side of the ditch (the south side of the lane).

The Red Regiment were the first to form up. Their commander, Wade, had fought well at Bridport against the Dorset militia, in June, on another occasion when Grey had failed to press home an attack with his cavalry. The Red Regiment were soon followed by the Yellow Regiment, under Edward Matthews. But neither regiment could be induced to attempt the crossing of the rhyne without support.

Turn left and follow the lane towards Bussex Farm. The royal army was across the rhyne on your right. Monmouth's men were formed up on your left.

For an hour and a half the two armies fired across the rhyne (this lane!). By now it was getting light. The situation was desperate. Monmouth's waggon drivers had fled the field taking much needed ammunition with them, and the Royal Artillery was causing havoc.

At the end of the lane is Bussex Farm.

Those of Monmouth's cavalry who had not fled the field with Grey had by now located the Upper Plungeon here, but there were too few of them to seize it from the king's troops. None of the rebel army could cross the rhyne. Though they continued the battle they, and it, were lost.

Turn right into Westonzoyland village, down Monmouth Road.

The village that night was packed with waggons, horses and drivers accompanying the royal field-guns that had been placed on the outskirts of the village.

From Monmouth Road turn left into Cheer Lane, then right into Gelosia Close. At the end, follow the footpath left. Bear right then left. It leads to the church. Go to the front of the church, on the main road.

Opposite the church is the site of Weston Court. It was here that Feversham set up his headquarters on Sunday and where he was sleeping as Monmouth's army crept through the dark. He was late onto the battlefield – tradition has it because he could not find his wig! Colonel Kirke, a senior Royalist officer, was asleep in the Vicarage, behind the church.

Go into the church.

After the battle some 500 rebels were crowded into the church; at least 79 wounded, of whom 5 died in here. Of the survivors, 22 were hanged without trial outside the church (4 in chains). These included, Monmouth's Dutch gunner and a deserter from the Somerset militia.

Follow the main road through the village in the direction of Bridgwater. Stop on the western edge of Westonzoyland, on a small bridge. Looking right is the spot where 18 guns were sited to guard the approach from Bridgwater. Walk on along the road for about 50 metres; there is no pavement. Pass a cemetery on the left and, shortly after this Penzoy Drove leaves the road on the right.

Go up the drove. This track marks the approximate line of the Bussex Rhyne, where it ran down to the west of Westonzoyland.

Between this track (the Bussex Rhyne) and the village, on the right, was the soon to be infamous Colonel Kirke, with the Queen Dowager's Regiment of Foot; the soldiers ironically called Kirke's 'Lambs'. Beyond him, to the north, were the Queen Consort's Regiment of Foot commanded by Lieutenant-Colonel Charles Churchill.

Move on up the track and stop by a Wessex Water installation.

As Monmouth's army battled with the enemy that they could not reach, Kirke moved his soldiers away from the southern end of the Bussex Rhyne, on our right, to reinforce the royal troops near Bussex Farm.

Just to the left here was the site of Pitzoy Pound. Here a picket of royal musketeers had been stationed to warn of any attack on this quarter of the defences. They had nothing to fear.

Walk on to where a ruined building is in the field to the left.

This is approximately the site of the Lower Plungeon – another crossing point of the Bussex Rhyne. At first light the Horse Guards crossed it, coming from the right. They galloped north and charged into the flank of Monmouth's shaken army. At the same time troopers of the Blues crossed the Upper Plungeon.

Walk on up the drove. Just before it bends right, go through a gate on the left. Walk across the field to the gap in the hedge directly ahead. Turn right, beyond the gap, and keep the hedge on your right until you meet the Chedzoy New Cut – a drainage channel not existing in 1685. Cross it by the metal bridge on the left. Walk ahead keeping the hedge on your right. Stop where you meet the course of a track in front of you.

Monmouth had long since left the battlefield but his men were still dying, as his broken army fell back from Westonzoyland. Wade managed to hold some of his regiment together, falling back to the shelter of a ditch. Here the king's cavalry fell on them and scattered them. Some succeeded in crossing and marched back to Bridgwater. Elsewhere others were running for their lives.

Where you are now standing is the southern end of what was, in 1685, Langmoor Rhyne. It is now traced in the track curving from right to left. Here, according to Rev Paschall of Chedzoy, 42 rebels were caught and cut down. Follow the track round to the left, to Fowler's plot.

In 1685 the land to the right was the enclosed East Field, planted with corn for the villagers of Chedzoy. The drainage ditches and slight elevation (along with a belt of meadow) separated it from the open expanse of rough grazing, reed beds and water courses of the open moor to your left.

It was into these corn fields, on your right, that the royal army pursued the retreating men. It was now daylight and the slaughter was immense.

The track winds to a metal gate and then bends right. Follow it to the hamlet of Fowler's Plot.

Contemporary reports claim that around 700 rebels had died in the battle, with about 300 captured, while the royal army lost 27 dead and about 200 wounded.

With the battle over the reprisals began. Captured rebels were hanged without trial at Westonzoyland. The Wiltshire militia hanged several rebels – at Glastonbury and Wells – as they marched home. Others were hanged near the battlefield the next day.

Feversham took some prisoners to Bridgwater – on carts, or in chains – while Kirke and his 'Lambs' continued the work of hunting and hanging rebels without trial. A number were hanged in Bridgwater and Taunton, while Monmouth himself fled to the Mendip village of Downside. From there he headed for the New Forest, where on July 8th he was found sleeping in a ditch near Ringwood by members of the Sussex militia. On July 15th he was beheaded on Tower Hill. It took five bloody blows, with an axe too blunt for the task.

The Sedgemoor Memorial.

At Fowler's Plot, turn right onto the road, which winds back to Chedzoy.

Terrible as the immediate vengeance was on his followers, what has remained vivid and raw in West Country folklore is the 'Bloody Assize' that followed. Some 1, 500 were tried by Judge Jeffreys in the Autumn Assizes. More than 300 were hanged, drawn and quartered. Some 900 were sentenced to be transported to the West Indies.

The memory of these men and their suffering is still real in the West Country. I was told of it, by my own father, in north Somerset when I was a child. Here I would like to record the names of members of my family who went with Monmouth; men executed, or accused of treason by their parish constables:

Charles Chappell – executed at Keynsham, 1685.
John Whittock, of Rode – in Monmouth's army, fate unknown.
Thomas Whittock, of Frome – in Monmouth's army, fate unknown.

Camerton, Coalmines and a Suicide

Camerton church – Carlingcott – Carlingcott 'batch' and mine –
disused railway and Somerset Coal Canal – Camerton 'batch' and
mine – Camerton Court – Camerton church

This walk of just under 4 miles is set in the heart of the Somerset coalfield amid relics of Somerset's recent industrial past in a strikingly rural setting. In its short distance a medieval church, sites of industrial archaeology, a splendid country residence and gardens are woven together in the landscape. There is also a local tragedy.

Time: Two hours.

Starting point: Camerton parish church. (Grid ref: 685 575).

Facilities: There are few facilities in Camerton. Nearby Radstock, 2 miles, offers more.

Problems: None This is an exceptionally well marked walk.

Background: This walk visits a variety of sites associated with coal mining in north Somerset, which expanded greatly after 1763 and lasted, in Camerton, until 1950. To assist in the movement of coal the Somerset Coal Canal was constructed to link with the Kennet and Avon Canal at Dundas, south-east of Bath, and a number of tramways and later railways were constructed. Evidence for all of these can be seen on this walk.

The walk offers excellent views of the valley of the Cam Brook and these contrast with the more secluded sections beside the abandoned railway and canal and the now wooded coal tips, or 'batches'.

Any visit to Camerton is incomplete without mentioning the Rev. John Skinner, rector of Camerton from 1800 until 1839. A lonely, stern, yet well-meaning and sensitive man, his journal records his fascination with archaeology, his disputes with the Methodists and miners in the village, his difficulties with his children, problems in relationships with the Lady of the Manor and, eventually, his complete isolation and despair. In 1839 he shot himself in the woods near the rectory.

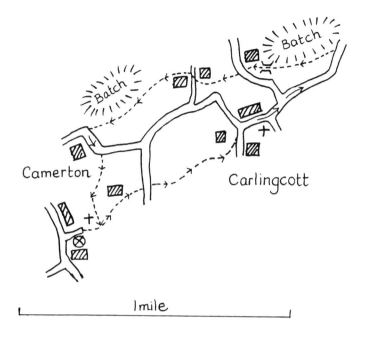

Directions

Park in the car park by the parish church. The church and then the car park are signed off the road through Camerton, linking the A367 and B3115. From the car park walk through to the church.

The house beyond the high wall to the left is the old rectory of Camerton (the present rectory is the modern house up the slope beside the car park). When Skinner lived in it the rectory backed onto the grounds of Camerton House (the present Camerton Court being a later construction). His relations were poor with the then lord of the manor, James Stephens and, after Stephens's death in 1817, with his daughter and heiress Mrs Anne Jarrett. According to Skinner's journal, it was her peacocks which disturbed the sleep of a man already isolated and mentally fragile.

Walk on into the churchyard and down to the church.

The church is first mentioned in 1336 as a chantry of St John the Baptist belonging to Glastonbury Abbey. However, there was

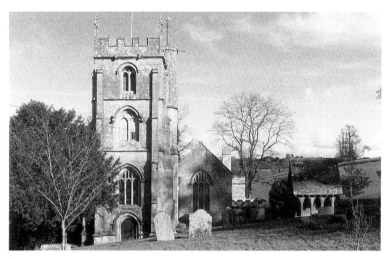

Camerton Church.

clearly a church here before this, as a record of 1292 refers to a rector.

Walking down to the main door, look at the figures carved above the west door of the tower: a woman with prayer beads, a monk with a musical instrument, a grinning cat, a dog and monkeys! On the north side of the tower there is an even stranger assortment – elephant, rhinoceros, toads and a monk!

Inside are two large monuments to the Carew family, dated 1640 and 1683. The women wear fine ruffed dresses; the men are in ruffs and armour. They were once brightly painted and the breeches of Sir John Carew the elder (d.1640) still show red paint, as does the pillow beneath the head of his son, on the other monument (d.1683).

Outside the church door, turn right and make for the gateway in the bottom corner of the churchyard. Go through it and into the field, keeping the fence to your left.

On the left are the gardens and ornamental lake of Camerton Court, which stands opposite you on the other side of a shallow valley.

At the end of the fence aim for the gate forward and left at the bottom of the slope. Cross the stile by the gate, cross the road and enter the field opposite by the stile. Walk up the slope, keeping a line of telegraph poles to your left and aiming towards the left hand edge of the hedge on the ridge.

On the ridge look back for views of Camerton Court and church and the volcano-like shape of the coal slagheap, or 'batch', to the right. Notice how the hill between the house and batch totally shielded the gentry from the sight of the industrial activity in the valley of the Cam Brook.

Aim for the gate in the right hand corner of the field ahead. Go into the lane and follow it. Notice how the lane is flanked by coppiced hazel, now no longer managed.

Follow the lane through a second gate (beware of mud). The track passes houses on the left and reaches a metalled road. This is the small village of Carlingcott, meaning 'The Cottage of Cridela's people', which as late as the 1830s was still regularly called Cridlingcot, revealing its original name. Turn left onto the road. Follow the road past another joining it from the left, by a telephone box. Keep straight on, past a row of miners' cottages on the left and the Methodist church on the right.

This church was built in 1851 to serve the nonconformist workers here (and, incidentally, later preached in by my father). John Skinner records (in August 1822) attempts to persuade Methodists at Carlingcott to return to the Anglican church, but commented 'It is throwing time away to attempt converting people of this persuasion'.

Former miners' cottages at Carlingcott.

A 'batch', or coal spoil heap, north of Camerton in the Cam Brook valley.

Carry on downhill past Stone Age Lane which joins the road from the left. Notice the 'batch', rising on the left, with the coal show-ing through the grass.The road bears gently left with Splott Farm ahead. Turn sharp left off the road onto a gravel track. Follow this and skirt the foot of the batch, with the Cam Brook flowing below you on the right. Two springs cross the path and the second is a miniature cascade as it breaks out of the rocks.

The spoil heap is from the colliery at Dunkerton, to the east, which was opened in 1905 and closed in 1925. It became the largest colliery in the area but had a bad safety record and in the winter of 1908-09 was the scene of strikes and rioting.

Use the footbridge to cross the Cam Brook and follow the path into a field. The Cam Brook is now on your left and a vineyard on the slope on your right. The path meets a road. Turn right onto the road and, after 20 metres, turn left into a field, opposite Stone Edge Cottage. Walk ahead and to the right, past a ruined cottage on the left, to the stile in the hedge. Cross the stile and go up the slope, using the rough steps. Follow the path to the left. On your right a disused railway is terraced into the hillside.

The railway here runs on the south side of the Somerset Coal Canal. A branch line of the GWR, it was known as the Camerton and Limpley Stoke Railway and was opened in 1910. Passenger services ended in 1915 but the railway itself was not shut until 1951. The towpath and bed of the canal, beyond the railway embankment, is well preserved.

On this stretch of path there is also a fine view down to the left onto Carlingcott Mill. There was a mill here (possibly on this same spot) when the Domesday Book was compiled in 1086. In the early 19th century, John Skinner records the marriage of its miller to a very pregnant bride.

Follow the path to a way-marked post and turn right. Go up the steps and cross the line of the railway, to a metal stile on the left. This is Sellar's Stile with a detached house just beyond the stile.

Between the site of the house and the rising slope ran a section of the 10½ mile long Dunkerton arm of the Somerset Coal Canal. It followed the same line as the railway along the edge of the hill but on the northern side of the track. At this point, as the railway carried on ahead, it turned north and followed the curve of the hill. Work on the canal began in 1794 and the waterway – which linked with the Kennet and Avon Canal – was opened in 1805. A southern branch to Radstock was finally abandoned in favour of a tramroad railway in 1815.

The canal was eventually defeated by competition from the railway and in 1898 it closed. Little can be seen of it now but a remarkable section survives in the back garden of the house here (NOT a public right of way) as a deep trench, some 6 metres wide and 2 metres deep. Beneath the grass, the puddled clay of its bottom still holds water. After torrential rain this section still fills with sufficient water to carry a small coal barge.

To get a better view of the course of the canal, take the footpath up the hill for about 30 metres, keeping the house at Sellar's Stile on your left. Looking down, to the left, a section of canal can be seen before it is lost in the curve of the hill.

It is difficult now to imagine its former splendour, when John Skinner took a party along it on a hired coal barge in June 1822: 'Passing the 'Swan' at Dunkerton the Camerton band came on board and played marches and Scotch airs the whole way home. The music and the dressed-out canal barge attracted multitudes who followed our course along the banks of the canal.'

Return to the stile. Cross it and follow the driveway from the house down to the road. As it curves right you leave the line of the railway but its embankment can plainly be seen continuing into the next field.

Camerton Colliery in about 1910.

Looking right, the line of the canal, terraced into the hillside, can be seen in a hedgeline running around the curved side of the hill. Bengrove Wood, on top of the hill, was the site of Cuckoo Pit (also known as Dunkerton Old Pit and Bengrove Pit).

At the junction with the lane turn right and quickly left, beyond a cottage. Follow this lane until you come to another cottage which should be skirted on its northern side. Beyond it cross a wooden stile on the left and walk down the slope and follow the southern foot of the 'batch'; between it and the river (back on the line of the railway).

Camerton 'batch', on the right was the spoil heap of Camerton New Pit, which lay beyond the 'batch' to the west. It operated from the early 19th century until 1950. Underground it was linked to Camerton Old Pit, which lay further to the west and which opened in the 1780s and shut in 1898. Both were initially owned by James Stephens, the lord of the manor of Camerton.

John Skinner records a multitude of accidents connected with the pits. One at Camerton Old Pit concerned a drunken collier – Aaron Horler – who tried to slide down the shaft rope. 'He fell down many fathoms and was dashed to pieces, his hands being much burned by the velocity with which the rope passed through them before he let go his hold.' On a different occasion a disaster was only avoided when a collier spotted that someone with a grudge had 'wilfully cut the rope, all but one twist.' The would-be killer was never caught, despite a two guinea reward offered by Skinner.

You soon come to a stile, where the line of the railway crosses the Cam Brook by a brick bridge. Go over the stile and on to a metalled road. At the road turn left. After 30 metres turn right through a stile into a field. (This is before the sign Wick Lane, by the remains of a brick built railway bridge and where a level-crossing gate is used as a drive gate by Purbeck House.) Three footpaths run from here. Take the middle one ahead and to the right of the pylon. Walking up the slope, aim for where the anti-rabbit hedge at the top of the slope meets the old hedgeline on the right. Go through the metal stile and keep the fence on your left. Go through a metal gate onto a pathway (sunken in parts) which crosses the drive and then the attractive gardens of Camerton Court. The path continues, crossed by two stone bridges, through the gardens and back to the church.

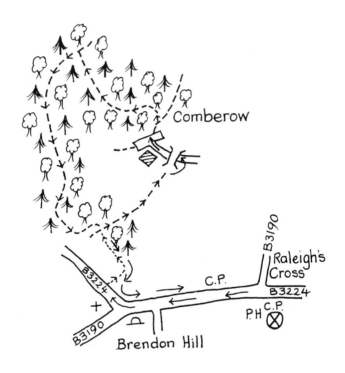

Comberow

B3190

Raleigh's Cross

B3224

C.P.

B3224

B3224

C.P.

P.H

C.P.

B3190

Brendon Hill

1 mile

Brendon Hill Iron Mines and the West Somerset Mineral Railway

Raleigh's Cross Inn – Brendon Hill – Incline Railway
Comberow – woods above Leigh Barton – Brendon Hill
Raleigh's Cross Inn

This walk of 5 miles is short but strenuous. However, the steep climb around the Incline Railway is through attractive woodland and offers an opportunity to explore an almost vanished episode in Somerset's industrial heritage.

Time: Three hours.

Starting Point: Either Raleigh's Cross pub (where the B3224 joins the B3190 on top of the Brendon Hills), or the small lay-by some 50 metres west along the B3190. (Grid ref: 039   344).

Facilities: None except the pub. Closest settlements are Washford, 5 miles, and Williton, 6 miles.

Problems: Strenuous hill climb. Short section on B-road.

Background: Dominated to the north by the dome of Croydon Hill, and by the high ridge which runs from Heath Poult Cross to Raleigh's Cross in the south, the Brendon Hills are almost a bridge between the Quantocks and Exmoor. They are one of the last places one expects to be reminded of industry and yet this walk explores an area which was once a hive of activity.

Iron ore was dug on the Brendons as early as the 13th century and by German miners, under the Tudors. It continued on this small scale until the 1850s, when deposits of iron ore began to be worked by a Welsh company, based in Ebbw Vale. Ore from the top of the Brendons was taken down to the little port of Watchet and from there was transported across the Bristol Channel to Newport. In 1855 an Act of Parliament paved the way for a railway to replace the horse drawn carts which had carried the ore to the coast. It opened in 1857, linking Watchet to Comberow, at the foot of the Brendons, via the valley of the Washford River.

In 1861 the terminus at Comberow was linked to the mines on the top of the Brendons by an incline railway . Soon some thirteen

The Raleigh's Cross Inn.

mines were in operation, but a collapse in trade caused their closure in 1879. There were later attempts to revive the industry but all failed.

Directions
Park at either Raleigh's Cross, or the lay-by to the west.

This inn was once a resting place for cattle drovers and packhorse men and takes its name from the stone cross, whose plinth still stands in front of the inn. A local tradition says it marks the spot where, in 1387, the body of Simon de Raleigh, the Lord of the Manor of Nettlecombe, rested on its way to burial, after he had died fighting in France.

Walk along the road to a point half a mile west of Raleigh's Cross. Stop where a minor road joins the B-road from the left, in sight of a small Methodist chapel ahead.

Over the hedge on the left and topped by trees is the Huish

Champflower barrow, a Bronze Age burial mound, 21 metres in diameter, which was partly excavated in 1903.

The 1000 or so miners who dug the iron ore lived in this area, and in time a small village sprang up named Brendon Hill. The owners of the mines were Nonconformists, so the village was tee-total. The settlement has now vanished, except for one of its churches.

Go on to the chapel situated at the junction of the B3190 and B3224 roads.

The village had three churches: a corrugated iron Anglican mission hall, a stable loft which served the Wesleyan Methodists and a meeting-place of the Bible Christians. This chapel, named Beulah, was built in 1861.

The village also had a store, a coal depot, a temperance hotel, even a Penny Bank. There was a midwife but no doctor, though the mining company paid for two surgeons to attend victims of accidents. Socially there was a Temperance Society, a teetotal fife and drum band, a choir and a Band of Hope.

Turn right downhill, at the chapel, signposted 'Wheddon Cross'. After 50 metres go through a gate into the field on the right. There is a small bridleway sign just inside the gate on the left. Walk forward with hedge on left. After 50 metres turn left, cross gate ahead and go forward, keeping the wood on your right. Go through the next gate and follow the path dropping steeply downhill. It reaches a gully. Stop here.

Beulah Methodist Chapel.

This was once part of the Incline Railway, which, running in its cutting (visible downhill), faced a one-in-four gradient to the summit. The incline cost £82, 000 to build – a huge sum of money in its day.

Turn right and follow the line of the abandoned railway down through its quarried cutting. Remains of sleepers and iron bolts can still be found. After a steep descent the line of the railway crosses a small road. Before this, turn off the line of the railway and drop down on the right to the road.

This is Comberow, the terminus of the Somerset Mineral Railway until the building of the incline, and the official terminus for passenger traffic. The first passenger train arrived here in 1865 accompanied by crowds and a fife and drum band. Passengers could ascend the incline but in a truck fitted with planks – and at their own risk!

Turn left and go through the tunnel. Turn right and look down the Washford valley.

At its peak the railway carried 19, 000 passengers a year. The closure of the mines hit the railway hard and it stopped running in 1898. Though there were later attempts to reopen sections, the line was finally shut in 1923.

Turn left, following the footpath signposted 'Raleigh's Cross via waterfall.' Walk up the sunken lane. Rising up the hill take the path (marked with a yellow arrow) going off steeply on the left. Follow the path along the side of the hill. It is marked by yellow spots on trees. As the path descends look left to where the cleft in the hill opposite marks the line of the railway you descended. Follow the path for about half a mile. It drops and rises twice before reaching a T-junction of paths with a signpost 'Raleigh's Cross and Leigh Barton.' Turn left, passing a ruined cottage on the left. Cross a spring and follow the path upwards (marked by blue spots). A path joins from the right but you carry on, bearing left. Pass small waterfall on right. Path bears left and continues up. Notice the wild raspberries in season. At the top of the slope take a right turn signed 'Raleigh's Cross'. The path rises steeply. Finally at the top of the slope the path turns sharply left and then veers right and descends to the top of the Incline Railway again. Retrace your steps to the start of the walk.

Unexpected Industry

Combwich – Parrett estuary – Stolford – view to
Hinkley Point nuclear power station – Stockland Bristol
Otterhampton – Combwich

This walk of 7 miles includes the broad estuary of the Parrett and the small villages and hamlets between it and the Bristol Channel. In this isolated area there are surprising examples of the intrusion of modern industry into a rural corner of Somerset – 19th century brickworks and a 20th century nuclear power station – as well as more traditional coastal livelihoods.

Time: 3 ½ hours.

Starting point: Combwich Village Green. In gravel lay-by beside the river. Near Anchor Pub. (Grid ref: 261 424).

Facilities: Pubs and village stores.

Problems: None.

Background: This stretch of coast between the estuary of the River Parrett and Stogursey is a little explored part of Somerset. Yet its flat marshlands and deserted shores offer a contrast to the uplands and rolling farmland enjoyed on some of the other walks.

It is a land mostly frequented by sea-birds and wildfowl, fishermen and cattle; of single track lanes with marshland and flat fields spreading on either side. Windmills once dotted the landscape and the industry that now dominates its open views is also ironically a power generator. The huge bulk of Hinkley Point nuclear station rises in towering squareness beside the dark sea.

Directions
Park in the gravel lay-by beside the river, on Combwich Village Green.

Combwich is actually pronounced 'Cummidge' and was a small port in the Roman period. It was probably not large enough to be a 'town' but probably an outlet for goods; linking the area west of the Parrett with South Wales. In the later Saxon period it probably kept this role, with its trade controlled from the royal administrative centre at Cannington.

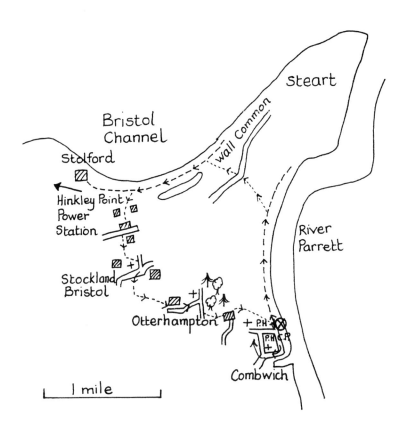

Facing the river, turn right and walk down the road, 20 metres to the next lay-by on the left. Go to the edge of the bank. There is a view of the TV mast across the channel which flows into the Parrett.

In the Middle Ages the trade of Combwich was controlled from Bridgwater, its powerful neighbour up the river. Until about 100 years ago the muddy waters of the Parrett, once known as Combwich Passage, could be forded. The base of the ford was formed from blocks of blue lias stones and there is evidence that even wheeled traffic could cross.

There are local traditions claiming that the River Parrett drowns in turn a man, a women and a child per year. Local folk-rhymes recall the greed of this river for human lives:

'Where's the farmer?' says the pump. 'Where's the mare?' says the well. 'I can tell you,' says the river. 'They do shiver-shake in Hell.'

Look down into the side-channel in front of you.

This is Combwich Pill, which drains into the Parrett and provided the first natural harbour. Excavations have found large amounts of Roman pottery on both sides of the Pill. The river emptying into the basin is a drainage ditch, the Putnell Rhyne. The wharf was built in 1958 to unload and move heavy machinery for building the nuclear power station at Hinkley Point.

Continue along the road. The Pill on your left is soon behind a new stone wall.

The main industry in the 19th century was the making of bricks and tiles. These were used in the immediate area and were also exported. The brickyard was sited on the other side of the Pill and operated from 1832 until the 1930s.

Walk on until the road reaches a T-junction. Turn right up Church Hill.

Half way up the hill is the parish church. There was a church here in the 14th century but the present one is Victorian.

Continue uphill and stop at the next T-Junction. Look left.

Bethel Congregational Chapel was built in 1838. It was originally a Mariners Christian Chapel and reminds us of the importance of the shipping trade to this small town in the 19th century and earlier.

Turn right downhill into Ship Lane. Go past the Old Ship pub on the left. At the bottom of the hill, just beyond Ship Orchard Villa, turn left onto a bridleway. The Parrett is on your right.

The Parrett estuary between Combwich and Steart was guarded by cannon in the 1580s to protect Bridgwater from Spanish attack. The attack never came but a map of 1586 shows the guns in position.

Follow the bridleway. Ignore a footpath leaving on your left. Walk on until you go under powerlines and eventually the track ends in a metal gate with a sign 'Bridgwater Bay National Nature Reserve'. Look over the gate.

Ahead is Steart. The farms and cottages on this spur of land were always widely scattered. Some ships put into Steart Bay in the 19th century to avoid going on into Bridgwater.

The land ahead is the Steart Island National Nature Reserve, designated part of Bridgwater Bay National Nature Reserve in 1954. As well as being famous for its geese and other wildfowl, it is also the home to another unexpected industry. This time it is the cultivation of Spartina grass used to bind together sea defences. It was first planted on the Somerset coast in 1928 when plants were brought from Poole Harbour in Dorset.

Beyond the estuary mouth, the Steart Flats stretch for three miles of mud at low tide. The river runs in a winding, deep channel between the Flats and the Gore Sands which curve northwards along the coast.

Before the metal gate, go left ahead and into the field, crossing a drainage ditch. Turn diagonally left across the field towards gate in the far corner. Cross the gate and walk towards the right hand corner of the field ahead (note drainage channels in the field). On reaching a gate, by a drainage ditch, turn left and walk towards the left side of the mound of earth ahead (drainage ditch on right and Steart Hamlet in middle distance on right). Cross next gate, turn left to road. Cross the road and walk ahead into a field, keeping the hedge and drainage ditch on your left. Walk to the sea wall and admire the view of the Bristol Channel, Steepholm island, and the South Wales coast beyond.

The coast here at Stolford, with its wide tidal mudflats is fairly typical of the Bristol Channel coast. There is evidence that the area now off the coast was heavily forested in 2500 BC and that the sea level has risen steadily. To the west of Stolford the mudflats give way to low cliffs, flat rocks, and a huge area of pebble and shingle.

Turn left and walk along the sea wall. The path then follows the

Hinkley Point nuclear power station.

A fisherman on his 'mud-horse' at Stolford.

track to the left of the wall. Stop where the track rises onto an embankment.

Fishermen here still cross the mudflats on wooden sledges, to reach their nets. The sledges are called 'mud-horses' and spread the weight of the fishermen on their runners.

Traditional fishing methods here include basketwork weirs, called 'putchers' and nets hung over frames, called 'hangs', or 'netstalls'. The fish caught include shrimp, bass, cod, eel and mullet. As late as 1819 seaweed was gathered and sold as fuel, by the name of 'ore'.

Walk on along the track. Pass a lagoon on your left. After another 100 metres stop where the embanked track is crossed by another track. Look ahead to the power station.

Hinkley Point's first nuclear reactor was built between 1957 and 1965. The reactors use up to 270 million litres of water for cooling from the Bristol Channel per hour and the site employs 1400 people.

The square block nearest you is Hinkley Point B. It has two Advanced Gas Cooled Reactors, producing power since 1976.

The blue bulk of Hinkley Point A lies beyond it. It is a Magnox Reactor. It is planned to build Hinkley Point C beyond 'A'. If built, it will be a Pressurised Water Reactor capable of producing enough electricity for the whole of Devon and Somerset, or three cities the size of Bristol.

Turn left down off the embanked track. Go over the gate into the field. Turn right and aim for the gate. Before reaching this turn left and cross a drainage ditch and another gate. Cross a wooden gate ahead and the one beyond it. Aim for the metal gate in left side of field, opposite a pink house on the right side of the field. Go through the gate. Walk down the hedgerow, keeping it on the right. Hedge bears right and ahead is a gate between barns. Cross the small yard and next field to gate ahead. Walk ahead towards the farm, under power lines, via a poorly maintained footbridge. Cross two metal gates and go up to the right side of farm buildings into the yard. Turn right and immediately left after farmhouse.

The flat ground north of Stockland Bristol, visible ahead, is called Pederham Marsh. Fish weirs on the wet land here once provided jobs and food for the surrounding area.

Aim directly towards the church tower, following the line of telegraph poles. At the bottom of the slope cross the rhyne by the footbridge.

Crossing the South Brook, look out for herons in the meadows and drainage ditches. The area you are about to cross was the site of a small quarrying industry in the 16th and 17th centuries. There were also lime kilns here.

Go on towards the church, keeping the hedge on your left. Cross another footbridge and wooden gate and small stone bridge. Aim for church. Before the end of the field cross the stone wall on the left using a stile. The original village was once here and its remains can still be seen as earthworks in the field on the left. Walk ahead to gate and footpath sign.

Stockland Bristol is so named because it was a manor owned by the city of Bristol. Before this it was called Stockland Gaunts, as it belonged to Gaunt's Hospital, Bristol.

Turn right and walk up the road to the church.

The church was senior to the one at Otterhampton, whose church only became independent some time after 1377. The present church of St Mary Magdalene replaced an earlier one, incorporating only its 14th century font and pieces of a screen.

Take the signposted footpath opposite the church, up gravel path and to the left of the house. Go through a gate into the field. Walk down the hedge and cross the stile on the left.

The land south of Stockland, named Beaverland, was once arable and was still cultivated in strips as late as 1547. The higher land ahead used to be quarried for lime and building stone, while clay for bricks and tiles was dug from the low lying land around the hamlet.

Walk diagonally left towards the buildings. (Stockland Manor away on your right.) Go through the gate in the middle of the left side of the field. Turn right and walk down towards the buildings. Cross over footbridge by ash tree. Walk up the right side of a walled garden. At the end of the wall turn left into the lane. Walk down the lane, past the Old Rectory on the left.

The next building on the left is now called Manor Farm. It dates mostly from the late 17th century, with 19th century additions, but the farm here was first mentioned in 1316.

Otterhampton itself is first recorded in Domesday Book as a manor which, along with Cannington, encircled the estate at Combwich. Its name then was 'Otremetone' and contains the Old English word 'oter' (otter), a reminder of the marshlands which once surrounded it.

Walk to the church, on the left.

The church of All Saints probably dates from the 12th century but only the font survives from this early church. The hamlet is now tiny but there is evidence that more houses once stood around the church.

Walk on along the road to a T-junction. Turn right, signposted 'Cannington, Bridgwater' and walk uphill. Towards the crest of the hill, where a wood on the left approaches the road, turn left through a small wooden gate. Walk down the edge of the wood on your left. Go over a wooden fence and walk on. Drift to the right, keeping hedge on left. Go through a gate and over a stile ahead. Keep to the left of the barn and drop down through the farmyard, keeping the house on your right. Immediately beyond the farmhouse turn left and then right over an iron gate. Walk diagonally right to a gate below. Go through and forward to another gate in the wooden railings ahead. Keep the grass bank on your left and walk on. Turn left before a bungalow to reach the bridleway by the river. Turn right, walking back to Combwich ahead.